# THE ARMCHAIR BOOK OF GARDENS

*the* ARMCHAIR BOOK *of*

# GARDENS

*a miscellany*

## JANE BILLINGHURST

GREYSTONE BOOKS

D&M PUBLISHERS INC.

*Vancouver/Toronto*

*For Jeanne*

Selection and introductions copyright © 2011 by Jane Billinghurst

See Acknowledgments for copyright information
on individual selections and images

Every reasonable effort has been made to locate and acknowledge
the owners of copyrighted material reproduced in this volume.
The publishers welcome any information regarding errors or omissions.

11  12  13  14  15    5  4  3  2  1

Greystone Books
An imprint of D&M Publishers Inc.
2323 Quebec Street, Suite 201
Vancouver BC Canada V5T 4S7
www.greystonebooks.com

Cataloguing data available from Library and Archives Canada
ISBN 978-1-55365-392-9 (cloth)

Editing by Barbara Pulling
Copy editing by Eve Rickert
Design by Peter Cocking, Jessica Sullivan, and Naomi MacDougall
Printed and bound in China by C&C Offset Printing Co. Ltd.
Text printed on acid-free paper

We gratefully acknowledge the financial support of the Canada Council
for the Arts, the British Columbia Arts Council, the Province of
British Columbia through the Book Publishing Tax Credit, and the Government
of Canada through the Canada Book Fund for our publishing activities.

# CONTENTS

INTRODUCTION

Ever since the first person planted a seed, then watched pale shoots explode into green, humans have felt deeply connected to their gardens. Where survival depended on fruitful crops, gardens were a link to the divine. Demeter was the Greek goddess of the bountiful harvest; the Maya had the handsome young maize god, his hair glowing golden in the autumn light. As the earth blossomed into abundance, gardeners thanked the spirits for nurturing both their bodies and their souls. In the temple gardens at Assur, flower beds provided bright, fragrant offerings for the gods of the Assyrians. Desert dwellers corralled

< Arts and Crafts designer William Morris (1834–96)
wove the wonders of the garden into his fabrics.

1

water, planting trees to banish heat and offer respite. For ancient myth-makers, gardens were the calm at the center of a threatening world, oases that sheltered heroes during their travels. Many religions portray the garden as the closest place to paradise on Earth.

Through the centuries, in gardens protected by stone walls, fences, and hedges, people have shaped the natural environment to meet their needs, pursue their desires, and reflect their values. Mughal emperors favored geometric patterns, with whispering water, heady fragrances, and luscious fruit conjuring up visions of the world they hoped to enter after death. Le Nôtre laid out the grand avenues of the Sun King's gardens at Versailles as a testament to human supremacy over Nature. Chinese scholars looked for rocks sculpted by currents deep in Lake Tai, seeking to bring the forces of Tao into their gardens. Healers everywhere cultivated medicinal herbs to treat the sick.

From the beginning, gardens have inspired imaginative responses, and not only from those who labor to create them. Using brush and paint, European botanical observers meticulously recorded the hues, textures, and wonders of precious tulips from Turkey, startling canna lilies from the West Indies, and exotic Abyssinian bananas. In all parts of the world, in thread, clay, and stone, on vases and vellum, artists have recreated the garden's intricate patterns, sweeping vistas, and shady corners. Poets, novelists, and memoirists have celebrated the garden's beauty, explored its mysteries, and lamented the frustrations it can bring. A creative exchange exists between those who actually make gardens and those who imagine them in other ways. In Italy,

Renaissance gardeners consulted Pliny's descriptions of his villa gardens and the poetry of Virgil when creating their extravagant villa gardens. The designers of Picturesque gardens in England—with their romantic wildness—looked to the landscape paintings of Salvatore Rosa for inspiration. William Morris, in 1881, likened embroidery to "gardening with silk and gold threads." The fabrics and wallpapers he designed transported the swirl of vines and the explosive colors of the garden into the home.

Above all, gardens promise us pleasure. A garden engages our senses as soon as we step into it. Sounds soothe, colors delight, tastes satisfy, textures arrest. Every time we visit a garden, the kaleidoscope

Le Jardin des Plantes in Paris, circa 1805

has shifted. A once-gentle stream now gushes in a torrent, scarlets have erupted from tightly closed buds, soft green has turned lustrously dark, tart flavors have mellowed, fragrance fills the air. Gardens, these places of social comment, aesthetic satisfaction, and emotional and spiritual connection, are also places where we quite simply *live*. We walk through them for exercise. We hold parties against backdrops of roses and honeysuckle. We sun ourselves amidst the petunias or curl up with a book in willow-patterned shade. No matter if it stretches for acres or is no bigger than a pocket handkerchief, the garden offers us joy, contemplative quiet, surprising revelations, and womblike protection.

When I moved to Washington State five years ago from the Canadian prairies, I had the luxury of starting my garden from scratch. I knew stately English landscape gardens from my youth, but the village where I spent my childhood had cottage gardens crammed with bachelor's buttons, forget-me-nots, and love-in-a-mist, hollyhocks shooting up through the chaos. These tightly planted, riotous spaces remain my favorite kind of garden. As soon as I had settled into my new home, I wanted hollyhocks—and holly and ivy, so that I could decorate the house at Christmas as we had when I was young. But hollyhocks suffer from rust in the Pacific Northwest, and holly and ivy escape to wreak havoc in the forest.

Instead, I learned to negotiate with my surroundings. Now, beyond a relatively manicured patio, my flower garden fades into a background of shrubs sturdy enough to enjoy regular pruning by deer. The shrubs give way to a disarray of hardhack, thimbleberry, and Nootka rose that I leave to the birds to seed. My garden is where I go on a summer evening to relax, surrounded by industrious bees and garter snakes soaking up the warmth of the day. I enjoy inviting people in to take a seat among the rhododendrons, the heathers, or the Japanese anemones, depending on the season. I have found a balance that works for me in my garden. At least for now.

Whenever I travel, gardens beckon. By accident or design, I have found myself in experimental gardens at Chaumont-sur-Loire; classical Chinese gardens in Suzhou and Shanghai; Japanese gardens in Portland, Oregon, and Albuquerque, New Mexico. William Kent's masterpiece of English landscape design at Rousham. The meticulously restored Gertrude Jekyll gardens at the Manor House at Upton Grey. Sonoran desert gardens in Arizona. Abandoned subsistence gardens on Village Island near Alert Bay, British Columbia. Gardens in New Zealand, Sweden, Chicago, California, and Montreal. Gardens great and small, intricate and simple. Each one expresses an idea, a point of view, a vision. And each, in its own way, is beautiful.

A lifetime isn't long enough to visit all the gardens we'd like to see. For me, the next best thing to being in a garden is to imagine being in one. In this book, I invite you to explore how others have envisioned, executed, and enjoyed the ever-seductive idea of the garden.

> The garden of Godwin King (1864–1948),
at Stonelands near West Hoathly, Sussex

## SHADES
## OF PARADISE

Somewhere in our collective consciousness, there exists a garden of dazzling, unimaginable beauty. Sparkling streams meander among trees of infinite abundance, in the shade of whose branches a person can relax into pure delight. No sight or sound from the outside world intrudes. The vibrant colors and heady fragrances invite all who enter to immerse themselves in this perfect place. Human frailties drift away as the garden whispers promises of eternity. This paradise haunts the edges of our lives—lost, yet to be found, or awaiting us after death—its likeness captured in cuneiform characters pressed into

< The prophet Enoch seated in a garden in Paradise

clay tablets, Islamic script etched in camel bone, Latin letters inked onto vellum, and Chinese ideographs brushed onto scrolls of silk.

Through the ages, people have sought to replicate this paradise on Earth. In imperial China, the Han emperor Wudi, who ruled a century before the Common Era, ordered the construction of gardens featuring lakes, rocks, and islands—miniature worlds that, if beautiful enough, might tempt the Immortals from their distant mountain homes to take up residence in his empire, bringing with them the secret of eternal life. The ancient Greeks lived in a mountainous, parched land where gardens were a rarity. In Greek myth, heroes discover fertile gardens in the course of their travels. In these unexpected havens, the adventurer can rest and regain his strength before returning to his quest. The fourfold gardens, or *chahar bagh,* of the Islamic world are walled, rectangular spaces quartered by watercourses that meet at a central pool or viewing pavilion. Planted with fruit trees and fragrant flowers, these cool oases emphasize luxury and relaxation, reminding the faithful of the rewards to come in the next world.

Walled gardens in medieval Europe also made spiritual connections. The fountain in the centre of the *hortus conclusus*—or enclosed garden—symbolized the baptismal font. White Madonna lilies represented the Virgin Mary's purity, violets her humility, and red roses the blood of Christian martyrs. As the garden behind its wall was fruitful, so was the Virgin. The secular equivalent, the *hortus delicarium*, or garden of pleasure, was a space where cultural and intellectual diversions could be pursued away from the rigors of the world.

Walled or not, gardens allow chattering thoughts to be stilled and memories to unfold. Scents on the breeze lure the mind back to a time when senses were heightened and joys were sharp. Reminiscences of childhood often immortalize a lost Elysium, a time and place that evaporates in the onslaught of growing up. The gardens we encounter in later life may help us to reconnect with our former selves. Freed, however fleetingly, from the pressures of the present, we find respite in gardens that allow us glimpses of past and future paradises.

## The Garden of the Gods

· · ·

*In Mesopotamia in the third millennium* BCE, *Gilgamesh, king
of Uruk, makes an epic journey through Hades and on to the Garden of the
Gods, where the Tree of Life glitters in the sun to welcome him.*

AND LO! THE *gesdin* shining stands
With crystal branches in the golden sands,
In this immortal garden stands the Tree,
With trunk of gold, and beautiful to see,
Beside a sacred fount the tree is placed,
With emeralds and unknown gems is graced.

*Ishtar and Izdubar: The Epic of Babylon*

## *Rewards for the Faithful*

. . .

BUT FOR SUCH as fear the time when they will stand before (the
Judgment Seat of) their Lord, there will be two Gardens—
Then which of the favours of your Lord will ye deny?—
Containing all kinds (of trees and delights);—
Then which of the favours of your Lord will ye deny?—
In them (each) will be two Springs flowing (free);
Then which of the favours of your Lord will ye deny?—
In them will be Fruits of every kind, two and two.
Then which of the favours of your Lord will ye deny?—
They will recline on Carpets, whose inner linings will be of rich bro-
cade: the Fruit of the Gardens will be near (and easy of reach).
Then which of the favours of your Lord will ye deny?—
In them will be (Maidens), chaste, restraining their glances, whom no
man or Jinn before them has touched:—
Then which of the favours of your Lord will ye deny?—
Like unto Rubies and coral.

*Interpretation of the Holy Qur'an,*

*surah 55, verses 46–58*

# *Eden*

. . .

AND THE LORD God planted a garden eastward in Eden; and there he put the man whom he had formed.

And out of the ground made the LORD God to grow every tree that is pleasant to the sight, and good for food; the tree of life also in the midst of the garden, and the tree of knowledge of good and evil.

And a river went out of Eden to water the garden; and from thence it was parted, and became into four heads . . .

And the LORD God took the man, and put him into the garden of Eden to dress it and to keep it.

*The Bible, Genesis 2:8–15*

> Adam and Eve in a stylized Garden of Eden

## The Pure Land

· · ·

*In the scriptures of Pure Land Buddhism,*
*the spiritual teacher Gautama describes Sukhâvatî—the land*
*of bliss—to his favorite disciple, Ânanda.*

NOW, O ÂNANDA, that world Sukhâvatî is fragrant with several sweet-smelling scents, rich in manifold flowers and fruits, adorned with gem trees, and frequented by tribes of manifold sweet-voiced birds...

And, O Ânanda, the roots, trunks, branches, small branches, leaves, flowers, and fruits of all those trees are pleasant to touch, and fragrant. And, when those [trees] are moved by the wind, a sweet and delightful sound proceeds from them, never tiring, and never disagreeable to hear.

*The Sutra on the Buddha of Eternal Life*
*or the Larger Sukhâvatî-Vyûha*

## Sacred Grove of Kaśyapa

· · ·

*In the Indian drama Śakoontalá, written sometime between
the fourth and the sixth centuries, a king reconnects with his lost love
and their child in the sacred grove of the hermit Kaśyapa.*

IN SUCH A place as this do saints of earth
Long to complete their acts of penance; here,
Beneath the shade of everlasting trees,
Transplanted from the groves of Paradise,
May they inhale the balmy air, and need
No other nourishment; here may they bathe
In fountains sparkling with the golden dust
Of lilies; here, on jewelled slabs of marble,
In meditation rapt, may they recline;
Here, in the presence of celestial nymphs,
E'en passion's voice is powerless to move them.

KÁLIDÁSA (CA. FOURTH CENTURY)
*Śakoontalá*

## The Feast of Peaches

. . .

*Hsi Wang Mu, goddess of immortality, queen mother*
*of Paradise West, and owner of the heavenly peach garden,*
*often held peach banquets for the Immortals. Han emperor Wudi*
*(140–87 BCE) built extravagant gardens to tempt the*
*Immortals to visit so he could learn their secrets.*

HSI WANG MU'S palace is situated in the high mountains of the snowy K'un-lun. It is 1,000 *li* [about 333 miles] in circuit; a rampart of massive gold surrounds its battlements of precious stones. Its right wing rises on the edge of the Kingfishers' River. It is the usual abode of the Immortals, who are divided into seven special categories according to the colour of their garments—red, blue, black, violet, yellow, green, and "nature-colour." There is a marvellous fountain built of precious stones, where the periodical banquet of the Immortals is held. This feast is called P'an-t'ao Hui, "the Feast of Peaches." It takes place on the borders of the Yao Ch'ih, Lake of Gems, and is attended by both male and female Immortals. Besides several superfine meats, they are served with bears' paws, monkeys' lips, dragons' liver, phoenix marrow, and peaches gathered in the orchard, endowed with the mystic virtue of conferring longevity on all who have the good luck to taste them. It

> A plate from the *The Mustard Seed Garden Manual of Painting*, published in 1679 by the playwright Li Yu

was by these peaches that the date of the banquet was fixed. The tree
put forth leaves once every three thousand years, and it required three
thousand years after that for the fruit to ripen. These were Hsi Wang
Mu's birthdays, when all the Immortals assembled for the great feast,
"the occasion being more festive than solemn, for there was music on
invisible instruments, and songs not from mortal tongues."

E.T.C. WERNER

*Myths and Legends of China*

# The Garden of Alcinous

. . .

OUTSIDE THE GATE of the outer court there is a large garden of about four acres with a wall all round it. It is full of beautiful trees—pears, pomegranates, and the most delicious apples. There are luscious figs also, and olives in full growth. The fruits never rot nor fail all the year round, neither winter nor summer, for the air is so soft that a new crop ripens before the old has dropped. Pear grows on pear, apple on apple, and fig on fig, and so also with the grapes, for there is an excellent vineyard: on the level ground of a part of this, the grapes are being made into raisins; in another part they are being gathered; some are being trodden in the wine tubs, others further on have shed their blossom and are beginning to show fruit, others again are just changing colour. In the furthest part of the ground there are beautifully arranged beds of flowers that are in bloom all the year round. Two streams go through it, the one turned in ducts throughout the whole garden, while the other is carried under the ground of the outer court to the house itself, and the town's people draw water from it. Such, then, were the splendours with which the gods had endowed the house of king Alcinous.

HOMER

*The Odyssey*

## *Song of Solomon*

· · ·

A GARDEN INCLOSED is my sister, my spouse; a spring shut up, a
fountain sealed.

Thy plants are an orchard of pomegranates, with pleasant fruits;
camphire, with spikenard,

Spikenard and saffron; calamus and cinnamon, with all trees of
frankincense; myrrh and aloes, with all the chief spices;

A fountain of gardens, a well of living waters, and streams from
Lebanon.

Awake, O north wind; and come, thou south; blow upon my garden, that the spices thereof may flow out. Let my beloved come into
his garden, and eat his pleasant fruits.

*The Bible, Song of Solomon 4:12–16*

. . .

THE WALL WAS high, and built of hard
Rough stone. Close shut, and strongly
Barred,
Enclosing round a garden vast,
Wherein no swain had ever passed;
Beyond all doubt a place most fair.
And I most gladly entry there
Had made, and plenteous measure he
Of thanks had won who showed to me
How, helped by steps or ladder tall,
My feet might scale the high-build wall.
O joy of joys! O dear delight,
If 'twere but given to me that height
To climb, and such sweet joyance win
As surely might be found therein.
This garden was a safe retreat
For hosts of nesting birds, and sweet
Their piping sounded from the trees,
The glory of the place; the breeze
Was redolent of woodland song,
Nor shall I be convict of wrong
In saying that it shields perchance
Three times as many birds as France

Contains elsewhere. The harmony
Thereof could scarcely fail to be
Such as would cheer the saddest wight,
And wake his soul to sweet delight...

I noted that from side to side
The garden was nigh broad as wide,
And every angle duly squared.
The careful planter had not spared
To set of every kind of tree
That beareth fruit some two or three,
Or more perchance, except some few
Of evil sort...

Near by were placed
Almonds and gillyflower cloves,
Brought hither from hot Ind's far groves,
Dates, figs, and liquorice which deals
Contentment while misease it heals,
And wholesome aniseed's sweet spice,
And much-prized grains of paradise,
Nor must rare cinnamon be forgot,
Nor zedoary, which I wot
At end of great repasts men eat
In hope 'twill bring digestion meet...

Roebuck and deer strayed up and down
The mead, and troops of squirrels brown
The tree-boles scoured, which conies grey
Shot merrily in jocund play
Around their burrows on the fresh
And fragrant greensward, void of mesh.

Within the glades spring fountains clear:
No frog or newt e'er came anear
Their waters, but 'neath cooling shade
They gently courded. Mirth had made
Therefrom small channeled brooks to fling
Their waves with pleasant murmuring
In tiny tides. Bright green and lush
Around these sparkling streams, did push
The sweetest grass. There might one lie
Beside one's love, luxuriously
As though 'twere bed of down. The earth,
Made pregnant by the streams, gave birth
To thymy herbage and gay flowers,
And when drear winter frowns and lowers
In spots less genial, ever here
Things bud and burgeon through the year.
The violet, sweet of scent and hue,
The periwinkle's star of blue,

The golden kingcups burnished bright,
Mingled with pink-rimmed daisies white,
And varied flowers, blue, gold, and red,
The alleys, lawns and groves o'erspread,
As they by Nature's craft had been
Enamelled deftly on the green,                                    25
And all around where'er I went
Fresh blooms cast forth odorous scent.

GUILLAUME DE LORRIS AND

JEAN DE MEUN (CA. THIRTEENTH CENTURY)

*The Romance of the Rose*

. . .

SHE OPENED A door, and conducted them into a large saloon of wonderful structure. It was a dome of the most agreeable form, supported by a hundred pillars of marble, white as alabaster. The bases and chapiters of the pillars were adorned with four-footed beasts, and birds of various sorts, gilded. The carpet of this noble saloon consisted of one piece of cloth of gold, embroidered with bunches of roses in red and white silk; and the dome painted in the same manner, after

the Arabian fashion, presented to the mind one of the most charming objects. In every space between the columns was a little sofa adorned in the same manner, and great vessels of china, crystal, jasper, jet, porphyry, agate, and other precious materials, garnished with gold and jewels; in these spaces were also so many large windows, with balconies projecting breast high, fitted up as the sofas, and looking out into the most delicious garden; the walks were of little pebbles of different colours, of the same pattern as the carpet of the saloon; so that, looking upon the carpet within and without it seemed as if the dome and the garden with all its ornaments had been upon the same carpet. The prospect was, at the end of the walks, terminated by two canals of clear water, of the same circular figure as the dome, one of which being higher than the other, emptied its water into the lowermost, in form of a sheet; and curious pots of gilt brass, with flowers and shrubs, were set upon the banks of the canals at equal distances. Those walks lay betwixt great plots of ground planted with straight and bushy trees, where a thousand birds formed a melodious concert, and diverted the eye by flying about, and playing together, or fighting in the air.

*"The History of Aboulhassen,*
*Ali Ebn Becar, and Schemselnihar,*
*Favourite of Caliph Maroon Al Rusheed,"*
*in The Arabian Nights Entertainments*

< The sultan's palace, Istanbul

# Hortus Delicarium

. . .

*With the Black Death ravaging Florence in 1348,*
*Giovanni Boccaccio imagines a garden where people can pursue*
*cultured delights far from the chaos of the city.*

THEY HIED THEM to a walled garden adjoining the palace; which, the gate being opened, they entered, and wonder-struck by the beauty of the whole passed on to examine more attentively the several parts.

It was bordered and traversed in many parts by alleys, each very wide and straight as an arrow and roofed in with trellis of vines, which gave good promise of bearing clusters that year, and, being all in flower, dispersed such fragrance throughout the garden as blended with that exhaled by many another plant that grew therein made the garden seem redolent of all the spices that ever grew in the East. The sides of the alleys were all, as it were, walled in with roses white and red and jasmine; insomuch that there was no part of the garden but one might walk there not merely in the morning but at high noon in grateful shade and fragrance, completely screened from the sun.

As for the plants that were in the garden, 'twere long to enumerate them, to specify their sorts, to describe the order of their arrangement; enough, in brief, that there was abundance of every rarer species that our climate allows.

In the middle of the garden, a thing not less but much more to be commended than aught else, was a lawn of the finest turf, and so green that it seemed almost black, pranked with flowers of, perhaps, a thousand sorts, and girt about with the richest living verdure of orange-trees and cedars, which shewed not only flowers but fruits both new and old, and were no less grateful to the smell by their fragrance than to the eye by their shade.

In the middle of the lawn was a basin of whitest marble, graven with marvellous art; in the centre whereof—whether the spring were natural or artificial I know not—rose a column supporting a figure which sent forth a jet of water of such volume and to such an altitude that it fell, not without a delicious plash, into the basin in quantity amply sufficient to turn a mill-wheel.

The overflow was carried away from the lawn by a hidden conduit, and then, reemerging, was distributed through tiny channels, very fair and cunningly contrived, in such sort as to flow round the entire lawn, and by similar derivative channels to penetrate almost every part of the fair garden, until, re-uniting at a certain point, it issued thence, and, clear as crystal, slid down towards the plain, turning by the way two mill-wheels with extreme velocity to the no small profit of the lord.

The aspect of this garden, its fair order, the plants and the fountain and the rivulets that flowed from it, so charmed the ladies and the three young men that with one accord they affirmed that they knew not how it could receive any accession of beauty, or what other form could be given to Paradise, if it were to be planted on earth . . .

At length, however, they had enough of wandering about the garden and observing this thing and that: wherefore they repaired to the beautiful fountain, around which were ranged the tables, and there, after they had sung half-a-dozen songs and trod some measures, they sat them down, at the queen's command, to breakfast, which was served with all celerity and in fair and orderly manner, the viands being both good and delicate; whereby their spirits rose, and up they got, and betook themselves again to music and song and dance, and so sped the hours, until, as the heat increased, the queen deemed it time that whoso was so minded should go to sleep.

Some there were that did so; others were too charmed by the beauty of the place to think of leaving it; but tarried there, and, while the rest slept, amused themselves with reading romances or playing at chess or dice.

However, after none, there was a general levée; and, with faces laved and refreshed with cold water, they gathered by the queen's command upon the lawn, and, having sat them down in their wonted order by the fountain, waited for the story-telling to begin.

GIOVANNI BOCCACCIO (1313–75)

*The Decameron*

*Rosa lutea maxima flore pleno* <sup>IIII.</sup>

*Rosa pervincialis flore in cartto pleno* <sup>III.</sup>

*Rosa centifolia rubra.* <sup>I.</sup>

*Rosa prænestina variegata.* <sup>II.</sup>

# Rose-Scented Fairyland

· · ·

ON MY FIRST entering this bower, of fairy-land, (indeed I may call it the very garden of Beauty and the Beast!) I was struck with the appearance of two rose-trees, full fourteen feet high, laden with thousands of flowers, in every degree of expansion, and of a bloom and delicacy of scent, that imbued the whole atmosphere with the most exquisite perfume. Indeed, I believe that in no country of the world does the rose grow in such perfection as in Persia; in no country is it so cultivated, and prized by the natives. Their gardens and courts are crowded with its plants, their rooms ornamented with vases, filled with its gathered bunches, and every bath strewed with the full-blown flowers, plucked from the ever-replenished stems. Even the humblest individual, who pays a piece of copper money for a few whifs of a kalioun, feels a double enjoyment when he finds it stuck with a bud from his dear native tree! But in this delicious garden of Negauristan, the eye and the smell were not the only senses regaled by the presence of the rose. The ear was enchanted by the wild and beautiful notes of multitudes of nightingales, whose warblings seem to increase in melody and softness, with the un-folding of their favourite flowers.

SIR ROBERT KER PORTER (1777–1842)

*Travels in Georgia, Persia, Armenia, Ancient Babylonia, 1817–1820*

# My Kingdom

. . .

MAY 7TH.—I love my garden. I am writing in it now in the late afternoon loveliness, much interrupted by the mosquitoes and the temptation to look at all the glories of the new green leaves washed half an hour ago in a cold shower. Two owls are perched near me, and are carrying on a long conversation that I enjoy as much as any warbling of nightingales. The gentleman owl says ♪ ♪ ♪, and she answers from her tree a little way off, ♩ ♩ ♪, beautifully assenting to and completing her lord's remark, as becomes a properly constructed German she-owl. They say the same thing over and over again so emphatically that I think it must be something nasty about me; but I shall not let myself be frightened away by the sarcasm of owls.

This is less a garden than a wilderness. No one has lived in the house, much less in the garden, for twenty-five years, and it is such a pretty old place that the people who might have lived here and did not, deliberately preferring the horrors of a flat in a town, must have belonged to that vast number of eyeless and earless persons of whom the world seems chiefly composed. Noseless, too, though it does not sound pretty; but the greater part of my spring happiness is due to the scent of the wet earth and young leaves.

I am always happy (out of doors be it understood, for indoors there are servants and furniture), but in quite different ways, and my spring happiness bears no resemblance to my summer or autumn happiness, though it is not more intense, and there were days last winter when I

danced for sheer joy out in my frost-bound garden in spite of my years and children. But I did it behind a bush, having a due regard for the decencies . . .

We had been married five years before it struck us that we might as well make use of this place by coming down and living in it. Those five years were spent in a flat in a town, and during their whole interminable length I was perfectly miserable and perfectly healthy, which disposes of the ugly notion that has at times disturbed me that my happiness here is less due to the garden than to a good digestion. And while we were wasting our lives there, here was this dear place with dandelions up to the very door, all the paths grass-grown and completely effaced, in winter so lonely, with nobody but the north wind taking the least notice of it, and in May—in all those five lovely Mays—no one to look at the wonderful bird-cherries and still more wonderful masses of lilacs, everything glowing and blowing, the virginia creeper madder every year, until at last, in October, the very roof was wreathed with blood-red tresses, the owls and the squirrels and all the blessed little birds reigning supreme, and not a living creature ever entering the empty house except the snakes, which got into the habit during those silent years of wriggling up the south wall into the rooms on that side whenever the old housekeeper opened the windows. All that was here,—peace, and happiness, and a reasonable life,—and yet it never struck me to come and live in it. Looking back I am astonished, and can in no way account for the tardiness of my dis-

covery that here, in this far-away corner, was my kingdom of heaven. Indeed, so little did it enter my head to even use the place in summer, that I submitted to weeks of seaside life with all its horrors every year; until at last, in the early spring of last year, having come down for the opening of the village school, and wandering out afterwards into the bare and desolate garden, I don't know what smell of wet earth or rotting leaves brought back my childhood with a rush and all the happy days I had spent in a garden. Shall I ever forget that day? It was the beginning of my real life, my coming of age as it were, and entering into my kingdom.

ELIZABETH VON ARNIM (1866–1941)

*Elizabeth and Her German Garden*

POETICUS

COLLECTION OF NARCISSUS,
The Golden Glory of Spring.

# Perpetual Springtide

· · ·

CONTRASTED WITH THIS world... were the holidays spent each
spring during my father's absence abroad, with two cousins of his, two
maiden ladies of middle age. No powdered footmen or groom-of-the-
chambers, no grim housekeeper or still-room maids served in their
small house, standing in a garden behind stone walls, in an Oxford-
shire village, of which even the walls were thatched. The whole scene,
the elaborate late-gothic church—large as a cathedral and with a spire
too lofty even for so important a building as that—, round which the
little village, built of golden stone, its every house thatched and having
mullion windows, congregated with a curious perfection on the slopes
each side of a small stream, appeared to be set, not as at Blankney in
some eternal snowdrift of the senses, but in a perpetual springtide that
belonged, because of light and the perspective, because of the way the
golden walls and buildings with their roofs of thatch looked against
the landscape, and in spite of the fact that the country possessed hills,
to the Dutch seventeenth-century masters or to the Flemish paint-
ers of an earlier time. The light had a golden edge to it, refined, yet
ragged and hazy as the petals of giant sunflowers. And they, indeed,
would have seemed the flowers most appropriate to beauty of this
order, but my brother and I always arrived there in the season of primrose, daffodil and tulip. Then, the garden running down to the stream
developed a special pre-Raphaelite charm that only belongs to small
gardens in England, and, beyond that, to those situated by the side of

water; each blossom, though the flowers grew in drifts, seemed separately illumined, prospering in its own nimbus of life-giving spring sunshine. Every bird showed the arc of its flight, every feather, in blue or green or russet, startled you with the soft purity of its colour, every branch, every twig, every leaf now unfolding in lily and silver and pale rose, retained still its own entity, its individual value, had not yet entered into the full symphony of green. It was the instant of spring equivalent to that at a concert before the conductor takes his place, when every musician in an orchestra for a moment or two practices his own instrument.

Sacheverell and I would arrive in the evening, when the sun was staring in at the windows of the house; one cousin would be sitting on a painted bench against the wall, the cramped branches and coral-pink clustered cups of a japonica forming a background for her, while cousin Flora, the elder, would be carrying a trowel, or weeding, moving among the clusters of polyanthus, the complacent, fat faces of the double daisies, pink or red, or the anemones and narcissus which starred the grass, or she might be examining the apple-trees, their trunks white-coated with lime, that lifted foamy crests into the blue and humming air.

OSBERT SITWELL (1892–1969)

*The Scarlet Tree*

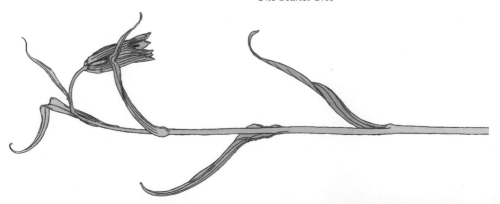

## *Joy of My Heart*
. . .

EVER SINCE I could remember anything, flowers have been like dear friends to me, comforters, inspirers, powers to uplift and to cheer. A lonely child, living on the lighthouse island ten miles away from the mainland, every blade of grass that sprang out of the ground, every humblest weed, was precious in my sight, and I began a little garden when not more than five years old... The first small bed at the lighthouse island contained only Marigolds, pot Marigolds, fire-colored blossoms which were the joy of my heart and the delight of my eyes. This scrap of garden, literally not more than a yard square, with its barbaric splendors of color, I worshiped...

When I planted the dry, brown seeds I noticed how they were shaped, like crescents, with a fine line of ornamental dots, a "beading" along the whole length of the centre,—from this crescent sprang the Marigold plant, each of whose flowers was like

"a mimic sun,
With ray-like florets round a disk-like face."

In my childish mind I pondered much on this fact of the crescent growing into the full-rayed orb. Many thoughts had I of all the flowers I knew; very dear were they, so that after I had gathered them I felt sorry, and I had a safe place between the rocks to which I carried them when they were withered, and hid them away from all eyes, they were so precious even then.

CELIA THAXTER (1835–94)
*An Island Garden*

IT TOOK A long time before I understood the satisfactions of giving away vegetables, but the pleasures of harvesting them I acquired immediately. A good visit to Grandma and Grandpa's was one on a day he hadn't already harvested. On these occasions I could barely wait for Grandpa to hand me a basket and dispatch me to the garden to start the picking. Alone was best—when Grandpa came along, he would invariably browbeat me about some fault in my technique, so I made sure to get out there before he finished small-talking with Mom. Ripe vegetables were magic to me. Unharvested, the garden bristled with possibility. I would quicken at the sight of a ripe tomato, sounding its redness from deep amidst the undifferentiated green. To lift a bean plant's hood of heart-shaped leaves and discover a clutch of long slender pods hanging underneath could make me catch my breath. Cradling the globe of a cantaloupe warmed in the sun, or pulling orange spears straight from his sandy soil—these were the keenest of pleasures, and even today in the garden they're accessible to me, dulled only slightly by familiarity.

At the time this pleasure had nothing to do with eating. I didn't like vegetables any better than most kids do (tomatoes I considered disgusting, acceptable only in the form of ketchup), yet there it was: the vegetable sublime. Probably I had absorbed my grandfather's reverence for produce, the sense that this was precious stuff and here

Poma amoris fructu
rubro.

it was, growing, for all purposes, on trees. I may have had no use for tomatoes and cucumbers, but the fact that adults did conferred value on them in my eyes. The vegetable garden in summer made an enchanted landscape, mined with hidden surprises, dabs of unexpected color and unlikely forms that my grandfather had taught me to regard as treasure. My favorite board game as a child was Candyland, in which throws of the dice advanced your man through a stupendous landscape of lollipop trees, milk-chocolate swamps, shrubs made of gumdrops. Candyland posited a version of nature that answered to every child's wish—a landscape hospitable in the extreme, which is one definition of a garden—and my grandfather's vegetable patch in summer offered a fair copy of that paradise.

MICHAEL POLLAN (1955–)

*Second Nature*

# *Patterns of Discovery*

. . .

FOUR OR FIVE years after I planted my labyrinth I began to accumulate more information on these various maze traditions, and I became especially interested in the labyrinth as a symbolic defense of a place, since at this time I found my own horizons shrinking as the world beyond my garden began to change.

Whereas in the past I used to range out over the wider world of Scratch Flat, poking my nose into every little corner and digging out more history of the place than anyone would care to know, the world of Scratch Flat began to change and my old haunts began to feel more cramped. Traffic increased on the road. Huge dump trucks lumbered by daily, carrying whole plots of earth from one place to another for the veritable assault of building that seemed to be going on in the town just to the north of the garden, where dark armies of developers began laying waste to the ancient civilizations of nature.

In the face of this, I determined to cultivate my garden even more than I had been. I found myself using the garden more and more as a walking place. I wanted to invent there a nation to defend myself from the outside world, and so, thinking to increase my walking grounds, I began designing winding paths all through the garden, a sort of unicursal, randomly patterned mizmaze that took up the whole acre or so and had various side loops that wandered off into grounds not strictly mine, the woods to the west, the lands of my ex-wife to the east, the overgrown old field to the north, and then back onto my land. All of these paths converged, flowed inward toward the entrance to the circular

In Norse mythology, the branches of the sacred ash overhang the universe.

maze, and then wound ever deeper, circling and splitting and turning and spiraling toward that singular, magical space, the ineffable center, the so-called goal, where according to tradition anything could happen.

The often-quoted advice in *Candide,* to cultivate your own garden, is actually delivered in reaction to all the calamitous events that Candide and his optimistic old fool of a tutor, Dr. Pangloss, had experienced. Candide and company, after many adventures and many losses, had ended up on a small property near Constantinople. Here they met an old Turkish gardener who lived quite well on his small holding, albeit surrounded by political chaos. He invited them to share his oranges and lemons, boiled cream and mocha coffee, all of which came from his own grounds. The old gardener knew nothing of local politics, nor the outside world, and yet lived happily. Pangloss and Candide returned to their land, taking him as their model, determined, finally, to settle there and grow their crops. Man was put in the Garden of Eden, Pangloss claimed, to work the land.

This idea of staying put, of digging in in the face of a world in chaos, suited my little garden projects quite well. Furthermore, the idea of the garden as a sanctuary, a place to begin, an Eden, still has meaning in our time, although for different reasons. We don't have to offset the unhoused *deserta* any more, the chaos of wilderness; we need to rediscover it. But the metaphor still works. The garden is not the end, it is the beginning, the place where you preserve the wild spirit that will save the world.

JOHN HANSON MITCHELL (1940—)

*The Wildest Place on Earth*

# NEGOTIATING WITH NATURE

$S$OME GARDENS are set apart from the landscapes in which they lie; others rest gently in their natural surroundings, making barely a scratch on the surface.

Where the surroundings are harsh and inhospitable, gardeners build walls around their plots to keep weather and marauders at bay. Within this enclosure, the gardener can indulge in exotic plants arranged in patterns of his or her own imagining. Where Nature is more benign, gardeners look outward, opening views to mountains or valleys beyond, diverting streams to ripple through the grounds, and

< Side paths in a Japanese strolling pond garden lead visitors to resting places where small wonders can be contemplated.

49

copying favorite local features within the garden itself. These gardeners use artifice to present Nature perfected, creating their impressions of the ideal landscape. In the Japanese text *Sakuteiki*, or "Records of Garden Making," at a thousand years old the oldest gardening treatise in the world, the author advises that, by making judicious choices from Nature's palette, the gardener can invite natural harmony into the life of the household. Other custodians of the land, inspired by the untamed beauty around them, simply trim back a bush here, encourage a wildflower there. A light touch, a secret pact between the gardener and the forces that hang on to life, and even the bare rock of a windswept island can be coaxed to fulfill unspoken desires.

For those who rely on their gardens to provide food, the pact made with Nature is a matter of survival. Precolumbian Mayan art depicts the god of maize rising from the earth with outstretched arms, and traditional peoples everywhere trod the fine line between experience and mystery to ensure plentiful harvests. Natural rhythms must also be observed. In sixteenth-century England, Thomas Tusser collected growing wisdom in his book *Five Hundred Points of Good Husbandrie:*

> White peason, both good for the pot and the purse,
> By sowing too timely, prove often the worse;
> Because they be tender, and hateth the cold,
> Prove March ere ye sow them, for being too bold.

A garden is a place where the temper of the land, the temper of the times, and the temper of the gardener intertwine. Above all else, in the balancing act between Nature and gardener, the gardener must remain vigilant. Whatever their original design or purpose, gardens left untended will explode with growth or dry up and blow away.

Plan of a flower garden and rosary in *Essays on Landscape Gardening and on Uniting Picturesque Effect with Rural Scenery*, by Richard Morris, 1825.

# Garden Magic in the Trobriand Islands

. . .

*As WWI raged in Europe, anthropologist Bronislaw
Malinowski recorded gardening practices on what are now
the Kiriwina Islands in Papua New Guinea.*

"THE BELLY OF my garden leavens,
The belly of my garden rises,
The belly of my garden reclines,
The belly of my garden grows to the size of a bush-hen's nest,
The belly of my garden grows like an ant-hill,
The belly of my garden rises and is bowed down,
The belly of my garden rises like the iron-wood palm,
The belly of my garden lies down,
The belly of my garden swells,
The belly of my garden swells with a child." . . .

After the *towosi* [garden magician] has thus chanted over all the
plots, the *okwala* ceremony is over. The gardens lie quiet, undisturbed
by human hand or digging-stick, covered with the leaves strewn over
them in sign of taboo, while under the influence of magic the tubers
mature rapidly underground.

BRONISLAW MALINOWSKI (1884–1942)
*Coral Gardens and Their Magic*

## Off Finnish Shores

. . .

SOPHIA KNEW THAT very small islands in the sea have turf instead of soil. The turf is mixed with seaweed and sand and invaluable bird droppings, which is why everything grows so well among the rocks. For a few weeks every year, there are flowers in every crack in the granite, and their colours are brighter than anywhere else in the whole country. But the poor people who live on the green islands in toward the mainland have to make do with ordinary gardens, where they put their children to work pulling weeds and carrying water until they are bent with toil. A small island, on the other hand, takes care of itself. It drinks melting snow and spring rain and, finally, dew, and if there is a drought, the island waits for the next summer and grows its flowers then instead. The flowers are used to it, and wait quietly in their roots. There's no need to feel sorry for the flowers, Grandmother said...

Grandmother was not always completely logical. Even though she knew there was no need to feel sorry for small islands, which can take care of themselves, she was very uneasy whenever there was a dry spell. In the evening she would make some excuse to go down to the marsh pond, where she had hidden a watering can under the alders, and she would scoop up the last dregs of water with a coffee cup. Then she would go around and splash a little water here and there on the plants she liked best, and then hide the can again. Every autumn, she collected wild seeds in a matchbox, and the last day on the island she would go around and plant them, no one knew where.

TOVE JANSSON (1914–2001)

*The Summer Book*

## Simple Scenes of Pure Nature

• • •

AT DORKING I swallowed a dish of tea, and got into a chaise for the Rookery, leaving my horse to bait.

The late proprietor of the place, Mr. Malthouse, found, I was told, a mere wilderness. The ground-plot is a valley between two woody hills. Part of the valley was watery. The hills were a thicket; and the water a bed of sedge. He has literally done nothing but remove *deformities,* and add *variety.* The water he has cleared, and formed into a lake: the woods he has opened in many places; and exhibited a variety of lawns, open groves, and close recesses. Everything is grand, simple, and uniform; the purest nature I ever met with in any improvement. At Stow, at Kew, at Painshill, you see the greatest profusion of expence. You everywhere see the hand of art: Nature never makes her excursions in such polished walks; plants her shrubberies, and her ever-greens in such artificial combinations; and brings vistas, and objects together with so much forced antithesis. But in all the beautiful sylvan scenes here exhibited nothing is introduced, but what nature herself might be supposed to create. Where you have a barren spot to improve, you must do the best you can: but certainly the simple scenes of pure nature have something ravishing in them, which art can never produce.

WILLIAM GILPIN (1724–1804)
*Rygate–Dorking, The Rookery, August 24, 1768*

# The Edge of the World

. . .

THE ROAD FROM the post-office came directly by our door, crossed the farmyard, and curved round this little pond, beyond which it began to climb the gentle swell of unbroken prairie to the west. There, along the western sky-line it skirted a great cornfield, much larger than any field I had ever seen. This cornfield, and the sorghum patch behind the barn, were the only broken land in sight. Everywhere, as far as the eye could reach, there was nothing but rough, shaggy, red grass, most of it as tall as I . . .

As I looked about me I felt that the grass was the country, as the water is the sea. The red of the grass made all the great prairie the colour of wine-stains, or of certain seaweeds when they are first washed up. And there was so much motion in it; the whole country seemed, somehow, to be running.

I had almost forgotten that I had a grandmother, when she came out, her sunbonnet on her head, a grain-sack in her hand, and asked me if I did not want to go to the garden with her to dig potatoes for dinner.

The garden, curiously enough, was a quarter of a mile from the house, and the way to it led up a shallow draw past the cattle corral. Grandmother called my attention to the stout hickory cane, tipped with copper, which hung by a leather thong from her belt. This, she said, was her rattlesnake cane. I must never go to the garden without a heavy stick or a corn-knife; she had killed a good many rattlers on her way back and forth. A little girl who lived on the Black Hawk road was bitten on the ankle and had been sick all summer.

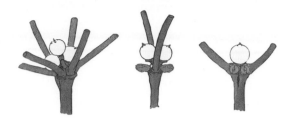

I can remember exactly how the country looked to me as I walked beside my grandmother along the faint wagon-tracks on that early September morning. Perhaps the glide of long railway travel was still with me, for more than anything else I felt motion in the landscape; in the fresh, easy-blowing morning wind, and in the earth itself, as if the shaggy grass were a sort of loose hide, and underneath it herds of wild buffalo were galloping, galloping. . .

Alone, I should never have found the garden—except, perhaps, for the big yellow pumpkins that lay about unprotected by their withering vines—and I felt very little interest in it when I got there. I wanted to walk straight on through the red grass and over the edge of the world, which could not be very far away. The light air about me told me that the world ended here: only the ground and sun and sky were left, and if one went a little farther there would be only sun and sky, and one would float off into them, like the tawny hawks which sailed over our heads making slow shadows on the grass. While grandmother took the pitchfork we found standing in one of the rows and dug potatoes, while I picked them up out of the soft brown earth and put them into the bag, I kept looking up at the hawks that were doing what I might so easily do.

When grandmother was ready to go, I said I would like to stay up there in the garden awhile.

She peered down at me from under her sunbonnet. "Aren't you afraid of snakes?"

"A little," I admitted, "but I'd like to stay, anyhow."

"Well, if you see one, don't have anything to do with him. The big yellow and brown ones won't hurt you; they're bull-snakes and help to keep the gophers down. Don't be scared if you see anything look out of that hole in the bank over there. That's a badger hole. He's about as big as a big 'possum, and his face is striped, black and white. He takes a chicken once in a while, but I won't let the men harm him. In a new country a body feels friendly to the animals. I like to have him come out and watch me when I'm at work."

Grandmother swung the bag of potatoes over her shoulder and went down the path, leaning forward a little. The road followed the windings of the draw; when she came to the first bend, she waved at me and disappeared. I was left alone with this new feeling of lightness and contentment.

I sat down in the middle of the garden, where snakes could scarcely approach unseen, and leaned my back against a warm yellow pumpkin. There were some ground-cherry bushes growing along the furrows, full of fruit. I turned back the papery triangular sheaths that protected the berries and ate a few. All about me giant grasshoppers, twice as big as any I had ever seen, were doing acrobatic feats among the dried vines. The gophers scurried up and down the ploughed ground. There in the sheltered draw-bottom the wind did not blow very hard, but I could hear it singing its humming tune up on the level, and I could see the tall grasses wave. The earth was warm under me, and warm as I crumbled it through my fingers. Queer little red bugs came out and moved in slow squadrons around me. Their backs were polished vermilion, with black spots. I kept as still as I could. Nothing happened. I did not expect anything to happen. I was something that lay under the sun and felt it, like the pumpkins, and I did not want to be anything more. I was entirely happy. Perhaps we feel like that when we die and become a part of something entire, whether it is sun and air, or goodness and knowledge. At any rate, that is happiness; to be dissolved into something complete and great. When it comes to one, it comes as naturally as sleep.

WILLA CATHER (1873–1947)
*My Ántonia*

Mount Fuji glimpsed through cherry blossom

## Gardening Wisdom

· · ·

A CERTAIN PERSON once said that man-made gardens can never exceed the beauty of nature. Travel throughout the country and one is certain to find a place of special beauty. However, there will surely also be several places nearby that hold no interest whatsoever. When people make gardens they should study only the best scenes as models. There is no need to include extraneous things.

TACHIBANA NO TOSHITSUNA (1028–94)

*Sakuteiki*

## Flowered Woods

. . .

I BEGAN TO roam ecstatically through this orchard thus metamorphosed;... the verdant grass, lush, but short and thick was mingled with wild thyme, balsam, garden thyme, marjoram, and other aromatic herbs. A thousand wild flowers shone there, among which the eye was surprised to detect a few garden varieties, which seemed to grow naturally with the others. From time to time I came upon dark thickets, as impervious to the sun's rays as the densest forest; these thickets were formed of trees of the most pliable wood, whose branches had been made to bend back to the ground, and take root, with an art similar to what the mangroves of America do naturally. In the more open places, I saw here and there without order or symmetry underbrush of rose, raspberry, and currant bushes, patches of lilac, hazel, elderberry, mockorange, broom, trifolium, which decked the earth while giving it a fallow appearance. I followed tortuous and irregular alleys bordered by these flowered woods, covered with thousands of garlands of Judean vine, creeper, hops, bindweed, Bryony, clematis, and other plants of that sort, among which honeysuckle and jasmine saw fit to mingle...

All these little walkways were bordered and crossed by clear, crystalline water, sometimes circulating through the grass and flowers in nearly imperceptible rivulets; sometimes in larger streams running over pure and dappled pebbles which made the water more sparkling... I now understand all the rest, I said to Julie: but these currents I see on every side... They come from there, she replied, pointing in the direction of the terrace of her garden. It is that same stream which at great cost supplies a fountain on the lawn which no one cares about. Monsieur de Wolmar does not wish to destroy it, out of respect for my father who built it; but what pleasure it gives us to come every day to watch the water we almost never go near in the garden running through this orchard! The fountain runs for outsiders, the stream flows here for us.

JEAN-JACQUES ROUSSEAU (1712–78)

*Julie, ou La Nouvelle Héloïse*

# A Landscape to Intoxicate the Heart

. . .

GENERALLY, IN THE construction of gardens, whether in the countryside or on the outskirts of a city, a secluded location is the best. In clearing woodland one should select and prune the tangled undergrowth; where a fine piece of natural scenery occurs one should make the most of it. Where there is a mountain torrent one may cultivate orchids and angelica together. Paths should be lined with the "three auspicious things" whose property it is to symbolize eternity. The surrounding wall should be concealed under creepers, and rooftops should emerge here and there above the tops of the trees. If you climb a tower on a hill-top to gaze into the distance, nothing but beauty will meet your eye; if you seek a secluded spot among the banks of bamboo, intoxication will flood your heart...

The view should include a watery expanse of many acres and contain the changing brilliance of the four seasons. The shadow of phoenix trees should cover the ground, the shade of pagoda trees pattern the walls. Willows should be set along the embankments, plum trees around the buildings; reeds should be planted among the bamboos. A long channel should be dug out for the stream. With hillsides as tapestries and mountains as screens, set up a thousand feet of emerald slopes; though man-made, they will look like something naturally created. Shadowy temples should appear through round windows, like a painting by the Younger Li. Lofty summits should be heaped up from rocks cut to look as if they were painted with slash strokes, uneven like the half-cliffs of Dachi. If you have a Buddhist monastery

as your neighbour, the chanting of Sanskrit will come to your ears; if distant mountain ranges can be included in the view, their fresh beauty is there for you to absorb. With the grey-violet of vaporous morning or pale evening mist, the cry of cranes will drift to your pillow. Among the white duckweed and red polygonum, flocks of gulls will gather beside your jetty. To see the mountains, ride on a bamboo litter; to visit the river, lean on an oaken staff.

JI CHENG (1582–CA. 1642)
*The Craft of Gardens*

The gardens of the Summer Palace, Beijing

## Rank Profusion

· · ·

THE OUTSKIRTS OF the garden in which Tess found herself had been left uncultivated for some years, and was now damp and rank with juicy grass which sent up mists of pollen at a touch; and with tall blooming weeds emitting offensive smells—weeds whose red and yellow and purple hues formed a polychrome as dazzling as that of cultivated flowers. She went stealthily as a cat through this profusion of growth, gathering cuckoo-spittle on her skirts, cracking snails that were underfoot, staining her hands with thistle-milk and slug slime, and rubbing off upon her naked arms sticky blights which, though snow-white on the apple-tree trunks, made madder stains on her skin.

THOMAS HARDY (1840–1928)

*Tess of the D'Urbervilles*

## Roadside Wild Things

. . .

I HAVE ALWAYS loved and encouraged rampant growth of easy plants, so that my only job is to hack out paths through them, seeding casually all the plants I love, many of them the roadside wild things. My favourite spots are the "wastelands." In Victoria I can tell you which vacant lot near Capital Iron has white and buff-coloured chicory, where you can easily find oyster plants (on the hillside where they park the city buses), where every shade of California poppies can be harvested, and which curve along the highway has easy-to-grow bachelor buttons in every colour.

I know many homestead sites and have raided them over the years for lilacs, cornflowers, ivies, various shades of bluebells and ground covers I have no name for. Almost everything in my yard either was here when I came or I brought it here with a long history behind it. Both Ron and I are very aware of how we feel about the yard when young children come and start stepping where they shouldn't. It looks like the wilds to them, but to us it is not.

I can tell you just where you can dig "martians," along which bends in the highway they grow. I monitor their progress each year. Some years they grow like monsters, making me wonder why the six o'clock news has not featured them as some outer space growth. Some years, the roads department chops them down before they are four feet tall, and they struggle to grow again, and do. I know all the spots where the teasel grows, including an old milk farm near Fulford Harbour on Saltspring Island. A feeling of warmth comes over me whenever I pass a spot where my plant friends used to grow.

CAROL GRAHAM CHUDLEY (1938–98) AND DOROTHY FIELD (1944–)

*Between Gardens*

# Transformation
· · ·

IN THE GARDEN, just beyond reach of where I sit on the veranda, is a round camellia tree covered with large, oval flower buds, pointed and green, protruding above a bed of dark, glossy leaves. The buds are fat like silkworm cocoons ready to burst, and one in particular seems right on the verge of opening, the dark-green sheath that wraps the flower eased open just enough to reveal a glimpse of pink within. It intrigues me and I wait patiently for the moment it will open, hoping I'll be watching when it does. It's not the flower I'm interested in, although I'm sure it will be beautiful. No, it's the moment that I await, the instant of opening, when the bud, fed to satisfaction on the nectar of the tree, will suddenly transform and blossom...

Gardens heighten nature's wild language by simplifying it, by sieving its complex messages to extract choice kernels: a subtle flow of time; a boundary that is and yet isn't; a balance born of imbalances. We amplify nature's messages when we build a garden and in turn the garden awakens us with those thoughts. Sitting and reflecting, drawn into the garden and out of ourselves, we find we are aware of familiar things in ways we weren't before, granted, if only for a brief moment, newborn eyes.

MARC PETER KEANE (1958–)

*The Art of Setting Stones*

---

< Magnolias predate the arrival of bees on this planet, and their sturdy flowers are designed to withstand pollination by beetles.

## Lost in Green

· · ·

I WAS SET down from the carrier's cart at the age of three; and there with a sense of bewilderment and terror my life in the village began.

The June grass, amongst which I stood, was taller than I was, and I wept. I had never been so close to grass before. It towered above me and all around me, each blade tattooed with tiger-skins of sunlight. It was knife-edged, dark, and a wicked green, thick as a forest and alive with grasshoppers that chirped and chattered and leapt through the air like monkeys.

I was lost and didn't know where to move. A tropic heat oozed up from the ground, rank with sharp odours of roots and nettles. Snow-clouds of elder-blossom banked in the sky, showering upon me the fumes and flakes of their sweet and giddy suffocation. High overhead ran frenzied larks, screaming, as though the sky were tearing apart.

For the first time in my life I was out of the sight of humans. For the first time in my life I was alone in a world whose behaviour I could neither predict nor fathom: a world of birds that squealed, of plants that stank, of insects that sprang without warning. I was lost and I did not expect to be found again. I put back my head and howled, and the sun hit me smartly on the face, like a bully.

From this daylight nightmare I was wakened, as from many another, by the appearance of my sisters. They came scrambling and calling up the steep rough bank, and parting the long grass found me.

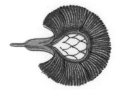

Faces of rose, familiar, living; huge shining faces hung up like shields between me and the sky; faces with grins and white teeth (some broken) to be conjured up like genii with a howl, brushing off terror with their broad scoldings and affection. They leaned over me—one, two, three—their mouths smeared with red currants and their hands dripping with juice.

"There, there, it's all right, don't you wail any more. Come down 'ome and we'll stuff you with currants."

And Marjorie, the eldest, lifted me into her long brown hair, and ran me jogging down the path and through the steep rose-filled garden, and set me down on the cottage doorstep, which was our home, though I couldn't believe it.

That was the day we came to the village, in the summer of the last year of the First World War. To a cottage that stood in a half-acre of garden on a steep bank above a lake; a cottage with three floors and a cellar and a treasure in the walls, with a pump and apple trees, syringa and strawberries, rooks in the chimneys, frogs in the cellar, mushrooms on the ceiling, and all for three and sixpence a week.

I don't know where I lived before then. My life began on the carrier's cart which brought me up the long slow hills to the village, and dumped me in the high grass, and lost me. I had ridden wrapped up in a Union Jack to protect me from the sun, and when I rolled out of it, and stood piping loud among the buzzing jungle of that summer bank, then, I feel, was I born. And to all the rest of us, the whole family of eight, it was the beginning of a life.

But on that first day we were all lost. Chaos was come in cartloads of furniture, and I crawled the kitchen floor through forests of upturned chair-legs and crystal fields of glass. We were washed up in a new land, and began to spread out searching its springs and treasures. The sisters spent the light of that first day stripping the fruit bushes in the garden. The currants were at their prime, clusters of red, black, and yellow berries all tangled up with wild roses. Here was bounty the girls had never known before, and they darted squawking from bush to bush, clawing the fruit like sparrows.

Our Mother too was distracted from duty, seduced by the rich wilderness of the garden so long abandoned. All day she trotted to and fro, flushed and garrulous, pouring flowers into every pot and jug she could find on the kitchen floor. Flowers from the garden, daisies from the bank, cow parsley, grasses, ferns, and leaves—they flowed in armfuls through the cottage door until its dim interior seemed entirely possessed by the world outside—a still green pool flooding with honeyed tides of summer.

I sat on the floor on a raft of muddles and gazed through the green window which was full of the rising garden. I saw the long black stockings of the girls, gaping with white flesh, kicking among the currant bushes. Every so often one of them would dart into the kitchen, cram my great mouth with handfuls of squashed berries, and run out again. And the more I got, the more I called for. It was like feeding a fat, young cuckoo.

LAURIE LEE (1914–97)
*Cider with Rosie*

# On Beans

· · ·

MEANWHILE MY BEANS, the length of whose rows, added together, was seven miles already planted, were impatient to be hoed, for the earliest had grown considerably before the latest were in the ground; indeed, they were not easily to be put off. What was the meaning of this so steady and self-respecting, this small Herculean labor, I knew not. I came to love my rows, my beans, though so many more than I wanted. They attached me to the earth, and so I got strength like Antæus. But why should I raise them? Only Heaven knows. This was my curious labor all summer,—to make this portion of the earth's surface, which had yielded only cinquefoil, blackberries, johnswort, and the like, before, sweet wild fruits and pleasant flowers, produce instead this pulse. What shall I learn of beans or beans of me? I cherish them, I hoe them, early and late I have an eye to them; and this is my day's work. It is a fine broad leaf to look on. My auxiliaries are the dews and rains which water this dry soil, and what fertility is in the soil itself, which for the most part is lean and effete. My enemies are worms, cool days, and most of all woodchucks. The last have nibbled for me a quarter of an acre clean. But what right had I to oust johnswort and the rest, and break up their ancient herb garden? Soon, however, the remaining beans will be too tough for them, and go forward to meet new foes. . .

Before yet any woodchuck or squirrel had run across the road, or the sun had got above the shrub-oaks, while all the dew was on,

though the farmers warned me against it,—I would advise you to do all your work if possible while the dew is on,—I began to level the ranks of haughty weeds in my beanfield and throw dust upon their heads. Early in the morning I worked barefooted, dabbling like a plastic artist in the dewy and crumbling sand, but later in the day the sun blistered my feet. There the sun lighted me to hoe beans, pacing slowly backward and forward over that yellow gravelly upland, between the long green rows, fifteen rods, the one end terminating in a shrub-oak copse where I could rest in the shade, the other in a blackberry field where the green berries deepened their tints by the time I had made another bout. Removing the weeds, putting fresh soil about the bean stems, and encouraging this weed which I had sown, making the yellow soil express its summer thought in bean leaves and blossoms rather than in wormwood and piper and millet grass, making the earth say beans instead of grass,—this was my daily work.

HENRY DAVID THOREAU (1817–62)

*Walden*

## GARDENS FOR
## BODY AND SOUL

---

**P**EOPLE HAVE long recognized the therapeutic properties of gardens. Repetitive work fatigues the body and hypnotizes the soul. At the end of the day, the satisfactions of aching muscles, sun-warmed fruit, and weed-free beds testify to time well spent. The Victorians wrote about the power of gardens to focus the mind on the mysterious ways of the Creator and to channel the energies of those who might be tempted to stray.

Gardens are not just to be worked in. They invite visitors and gardeners alike to slow down. Those who accept the invitation are drawn

---

< To work, to sleep, perchance to dream

to the water droplet nestled in a leaf of a lady's mantle, the yellow-dusted fuzz of a bumblebee backing out of a foxglove flower, the fragrance of lilac blossoms on the breeze. Careless of time, the dawdler reaches out to the softness of lamb's ears, crushes the fragrant thyme pushing out through a paving crack, and follows a tree-frog chirp to its red-eyed, green-legged source. Senses alert, those who linger are inexorably drawn into the popping, crackling, rustling life of the garden. Regular visitors observe the progress of green shoots in spring, drink in the intensifying riot of color in summer, and brush through flaming leaves at season's end, falling into the rhythm of the garden and its promises of surprise and rebirth.

## Royal Therapy in Persia

. . .

LYSANDER, IT SEEMS, had gone with presents sent by the Allies to Cyrus, who entertained him, and amongst other marks of courtesy showed him his "paradise" at Sardis. Lysander was astonished at the beauty of the trees within, all planted at equal intervals, the long straight rows of waving branches, the perfect regularity, the rectangular symmetry of the whole, and the many sweet scents which hung about them as they paced the park. In admiration he exclaimed to Cyrus: "All this beauty is marvellous enough, but what astonishes me still more is the talent of the artificer who mapped out and arranged for you the several parts of this fair scene." Cyrus was pleased by the remark, and said: "Know then, Lysander, it is I who measured and arranged it all. Some of the trees," he added, "I planted with my own hands." Then Lysander, regarding earnestly the speaker, when he saw the beauty of his apparel and perceived its fragrance, the splendour

also of the necklaces and armlets, and other ornaments which he wore, exclaimed: "What say you, Cyrus? did you with your own hands plant some of these trees?" whereat the other: "Does that surprise you, Lysander? I swear to you by Mithres, when in ordinary health I never dream of sitting down to supper without first practising some exercise of war or husbandry in the sweat of my brow, or venturing some strife of honour, as suits my mood." "On hearing this," said Lysander to his friend, "I could not help seizing him by the hand and exclaiming, 'Cyrus, you have indeed good right to be a happy man, since you are happy in being a good man.'"

XENOPHON (CA. 431–CA. 352 BCE)
*The Economist*

A ninth-century depiction of orchard maintenance in February

# Get a Garden!

· · ·

THOUGH A LIFE of retreat offers various joys,
None I think will compare with the time one employs
In the study of herbs, or in striving to gain
Some practical knowledge of nature's domain.
Get a garden! What kind you may get matters not,
Though the soil be light, friable, sandy and hot,
Or alternately heavy and rich with stiff clay;
Let it lie on a hill, or slope gently away
To the level, or sink in an overgrown dell—
Don't despair, it will serve to grow vegetables well!
Provided no sloth takes the edge of your zeal,
And you never permit yourself scornful to feel
Of the infinite pains a true gardener must take,
Or seek a short cut—the one fatal mistake!
And provided you have no objection to soil
And harden your hands with good open-air toil,
And are willing to push a full dung-barrow out
On the parched earth, and there spread its contents about.
The advice given here is no copy-book rule,
Picked up second-hand, read in books, learned at school,
But the fruit of hard labour and personal test
To which I have sacrificed pleasure and rest.

WALAFRID STRABO (CA. 808–849)

*Hortulus*

## The Meetest Place on Earth

. . .

ONE DIVINE ARGUMENT of the dignitie, and value of *Planting Fruit-trees*, and the *Art of Planting* may be this.

*It was Adam's imployment in his innocency to keepe, and order the Garden of Fruit-trees, Gen 2. 15. And the Lord God put him into the Garden of Eden to dresse it, and to keep it.*

God, who is wisdome it selfe, saw that a *Garden of Fruit-trees* was the meetest place upon all the Earth, for *Adam* to dwell in, even in his state of perfection: And therein assigned him *as imployment* for his greater delight, and pleasure: so that *this imployment,* as it is ancient, so it is honourable.

R.A. AUSTEN (CA. 1612–1676)
*The Spiritual Use of an Orchard*

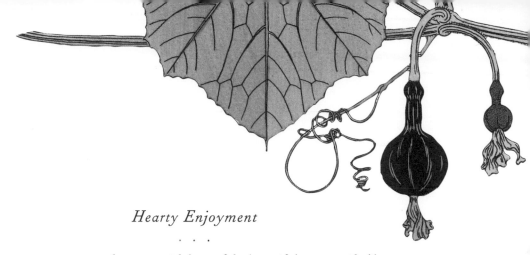

## Hearty Enjoyment

· · ·

BUT NOT MERELY the squeamish love of the beautiful was gratified by my toil in the kitchen garden. There was a hearty enjoyment, likewise, in observing the growth of the crook-necked winter squashes, from the first little bulb, with the withered blossom adhering to it, until they lay strewn upon the soil, big round fellows, hiding their heads beneath the leaves, but turning up their great, yellow rotundities to the noon-tide sun. Gazing at them, I felt that by my agency something worth living for had been done. A new substance had been born into the world. They were real and tangible existences, which the mind could seize hold of, and rejoice in. A cabbage, too,—especially the early Dutch cabbage, which swells to a monstrous circumference, until its ambitious heart often bursts asunder,—is a matter to be proud of when we can claim a share with the earth and sky in producing it. But, after all, the highest pleasure is reserved until these vegetable children of ours are smoking on the table, and we, like Saturn, make a meal of them.

NATHANIEL HAWTHORNE (1804–64)

*Mosses from an Old Manse*

NOW, IN SPRING gardeners are irresistibly drawn to their gardens; as soon as they lay the spoon down, they are on the beds, presenting their rumps to the splendid azure sky; here they crumble a warm clod between their fingers, there they push nearer the roots a weathered and precious piece of last year's dung, there they pull out a weed, and here they pick up a little stone; now they work up the soil round the strawberries, and in a moment they bend to some young lettuce, nose close to the earth, fondly tickling a fragile tuft of roots. In this position they enjoy spring, while over their behinds the sun describes his glorious circuit, the clouds swim, and the birds of heaven mate. Already the cherry buds are opening, young foliage is expanding with sweet tenderness, blackbirds sing like mad; then the gardener straightens himself, eases his back, and says thoughtfully: "In autumn I shall manure it thoroughly, and I shall add some sand."

But there is one moment when the gardener rises and straightens himself up to his full height; this is in the afternoon, when he administers the sacrament of water to his little garden. Then he stands, straight and almost noble, directing the jet of water from the mouth of the hydrant; the water rushes in a silver and kissing shower; out of the puffy soil wafts a perfumed breath of moisture, every little leaf is almost wildly green, and sparkles with an appetizing joy, so that a man might eat it. "So, and now it is enough," the gardener whispers

happily; he does not mean by "it" the little cherry-tree covered with buds, or the purple currant; he is thinking of the brown soil.

And, after the sun has set he sighs with deep content: "I have sweated to-day!"

KAREL ČAPEK (1890–1938)

*The Gardener's Year*

A German cottage garden, circa 1910

## A Kindly Benefactor

A FLOWER GARDEN is a great resource to a lady. We have, in our rather limited sphere, a good deal to suffer, and a good deal to make the best of, and, in each case, our minds seemed healed and mollified by the sight and smell of our gay and fragrant parterres. A flower, too, is a sermon—it preaches to our hearts and minds—it speaks to us loudly and powerfully of the tender love of our and its Creator—and it declares impressively also, this solemn and salutary truth, "man is as a flower of the field." We are taught, too, how wise, as well as how pleasant it is, to look for all we need spiritually and temporally from our heavenly Father.—"How much more shall he clothe you, oh ye of little faith." Thus in every way our garden is a kind of benefactor—it gives us moral health and physical health—pleasure and profit—recollection, and sometimes a blessed forgetfulness. I can truly say, that few moments are more exhilarating than that in which I unfold and arrange my large checked apron—plunge my hands into its ample pockets to find my knife, scissors, pack-thread, and old gloves, all of which you are sure to lose or mislay, if you do not keep them there; and snatching up my basket, rake, and trowel, hurry forth into my peaceful garden.

ROSA, 1848
*"My Flowers"*

89

< A country flower garden, 1894

# The Least Selfish of Social Pleasures

. . .

IT IS UNQUESTIONABLE that men of high moral attributes, rich and poor alike, are naturally drawn to gardening, and I believe it to be equally true that the pursuit of it, whether for profit or as a recreation, produces a love of order and a distaste for low and sordid pleasures. The physical exertion necessary for successful gardening is healthful to the body, and the interest arising from the ever-varying changes in the aspect of vegetables, fruits, and flowers is equally healthful to the mind, and this has a moral as well as an educational influence. The sequence of events is so rapid, so plain, so beautiful, that even the untutored mind can hardly help having forced upon its attention what we are accustomed to speak of as cause and effect. We sow the seed, and however limited our experience, upheld by hope, we rest assured that we shall see, and usually do see in succession, the germ, the plant, and in some cases the flower and the seed again. The habit of reflection is thus perhaps insensibly acquired and cultivated, and the moral nature is improved.

I would here ask you momentarily to contrast the moral influences likely to ensue from a recreation such as this, with those engendered by the too common practice of the cottager in separating himself from his family when his work is over, and resorting to the unhealthy atmosphere of a taproom and its surroundings. Once there, he too often spends his hard-earned wages in drinking and smoking to an extent which is both extravagant and harmful, and to which he is often

---

> The moral benefits of gardening

stimulated by conversations and amusements which are the reverse of healthful. Do not, however, let it be supposed that I am passing an unqualified condemnation on these luxuries and amusements; it is the abuse of them only that I would condemn. Let the cottager smoke his pipe, quaff his ale, and chat with his neighbors if so inclined in his garden plot and elsewhere. Labour creates thirst, physical exertion needs rest, and happy the man who can be content to assuage the one and enjoy the other under the healthy conditions of his own home or garden. Here, as in the ale-house, he may come in contact with men of his own age, men of the same mental caliber and social status, seeking one common aim, while his energies are aroused by the desire to do as well or better than his compeers, and as this is a kind of labour which naturally leads to healthy thinking while working, his whole nature is likely to be improved by the trains of thought awakened.

WILLIAM PAUL (1822–1905)

*Address to the Horticultural Congress in Oxford, July 21, 1870*

# *Finding Repose*

. . .

IN ALL MADRID there was no spot more beautiful or better regulated. It was laid out with the most exquisite taste; The choicest flowers adorned it in the height of luxuriance, and though artfully arranged, seemed only planted by the hand of Nature: Fountains, springing from basons of white Marble, cooled the air with perpetual showers; and the Walls were entirely covered by Jessamine, vines, and Honeysuckles. The hour now added to the beauty of the scene. The full Moon, ranging through a blue and cloudless sky, shed upon the trees a trembling luster, and the waters of the fountains sparkled in the silver beam: A gentle breeze breathed the fragrance of Orange-blossoms along the Alleys; and the Nightingale poured forth her melodious murmur from the shelter of an artificial wilderness. Thither the Abbot bent his steps.

In the bosom of this little Grove stood a rustic Grotto, formed in imitation of an Hermitage. The walls were constructed of roots of trees, and the interstices filled up with Moss and Ivy. Seats of Turf were placed on either side, and a natural Cascade fell from the Rock above. Buried in himself the Monk approached the spot. The universal calm had communicated itself to his bosom, and a voluptuous tranquility spread languor through his soul.

MATTHEW LEWIS (1775–1818)

*The Monk*

# *Journey*

. . .

I AM WITHDRAWING from the scourge of forty-five years of drinking. Two months ago I stumbled into a treatment centre for alcohol and drug addiction. Now, I am barely detoxed. Standing here among the sword ferns my senses seem to be thin glass, so acute at their edges I am afraid I will cut myself simply by touching the silicon edge of a bamboo leaf. The flicker's blade of beak as it slices into the apple makes me wince. My hands are pale animals. The smallest sounds, a junco flitting between viburnum leaves, a drop of water falling on the cedar deck, make me cringe. I can smell the bitter iron in the mosses on the apple tree's branches. My flesh at times is in agony, and I feel as if I have come out from some shadowed place into light for the first time. I feel, for the first time in years, alive.

The opal drop of water the chickadee drank is no different than the droplet at the tip of a bare apple tree bud that I lift my hand to. I extend my trembling finger and the water slides onto my fingernail. I lift it to my lips and take a sip of what was once fog. It is a single cold on the tip of my tongue. I feel I am some delicate creature come newly to this place for, though I know it well, I must learn again this small half-acre of land with its intricate beauties, its many arrangements of earth, air, water, and stone.

The garden begins with my body. I am this place, though I feel it at the most attenuated level imaginable. I am come alive again.

PATRICK LANE (1939–)

*There Is a Season*

# A Curtain of Green

. . .

EVERY DAY ONE summer in Larkin's Hill, it rained a little. The rain was a regular thing, and would come about two o'clock in the afternoon.

Onc day, almost as late as five o'clock, the sun was still shining. It seemed almost to spin in a tiny groove in the polished sky, and down below, in the trees along the street and in the rows of flower gardens in the town, every leaf reflected the sun from a hardness like a mirror surface. Nearly all the women sat in the windows of their houses, fanning and sighing, waiting for the rain.

Mrs. Larkin's garden was a large, densely grown plot running downhill behind the small white house where she lived alone now, since the death of her husband. The sun and the rain that beat down so heavily that summer had not kept her from working there daily. Now the intense light like a tweezers picked out her clumsy, small figure in its old pair of men's overalls rolled up at the sleeves and trousers, separated it from the thick leaves, and made it look strange and yellow as she worked with a hoe—over-vigorous, disreputable, and heedless.

Within its border of hedge, high like a wall, and visible only from the upstairs windows of the neighbors, the slanting, tangled garden, more and more over-abundant and confusing, must have become so familiar to Mrs. Larkin that quite possibly by now she was unable to conceive of any other place. Since the accident in which her husband was killed, she had never once been seen anywhere else. Every morning she might be observed walking slowly, almost timidly, out of the white house, wearing a pair of the untidy overalls, often with her hair streaming and tangled where she had neglected to comb it. She would wander about for a little while at first, uncertainly, deep among the plants and wet with their dew, and yet not quite putting out her hand to touch anything. And then a sort of sturdiness would possess her—stabilize her; she would stand still for a moment, as if a blindfold were being removed; and then she would kneel in the flowers and begin to work.

She worked without stopping, almost invisibly, submerged all day among the thick, irregular, sloping beds of plants. The servant would call her at dinnertime, and she would obey; but it was not until it was completely dark that she would truthfully give up her labor and with a drooping, submissive walk appear at the house, slowly opening the small low door at the back. Even the rain would bring only a pause to her. She would move to the shelter of the pear tree, which in mid-April hung heavily almost to the ground in brilliant full leaf, in the center of the garden.

EUDORA WELTY (1909–2001)
*"A Curtain of Green"*

# *Hope*

. . .

IT HAD ALWAYS been my dream to have a beautiful garden. In Clapham, as a small child, despite living in a second-floor flat and having no right to a small triangle of earth to the right of the main entrance, I had wheedled the tending of this small patch from our neighbours. It was to have been a herb garden. I spent my very meager pocket money on seeds for it. I brought cuttings of sage and thyme and rosemary from visits to friends with "proper" gardens. It was a triangle doomed to failure. Cars coming in and out of the adjacent car park failed to recognize its aesthetic potential and drove over it. By the time I was ten, it was reduced to a row of herbs with their backs to the red-brick wall and a bed of six-inch nails to protect them. The nails sank into the earth more willingly than any of the roots of my cuttings; and both my revenge and gardening were singularly ineffective.

So much of a subtropical landscape is a garden in itself that from day one at the *trapiche* I made grandiose plans for landscaping around the banana palms, lilies and mango trees, adding ornamental plants to create beds and shrubberies and, dearest to my heart, a herb garden. Whatever I planted, the beagles dug up. Sometimes, they ploughed over my seed-beds, and sometimes they allowed the seeds to germinate and grow into spindly seedlings before their digging and scattering began. Rose cuttings were a particular challenge to them. Beside the onslaught of my own dogs, the weeds and insects proliferated at a speed I had never dreamt of. When it rained, everything

rotted, then, with the dry season, everything wilted and died. I was stubbornly determined to persist with this garden despite all the evidence that I was fighting a losing battle.

Joanne also loved gardens. We had often spent our Sundays visiting the English ones that were open to the public and we were regular visitors to Kew. Telling her how well my garden was coming along was like telling her how well my marriage was. She was too far away to know any different and the simulacrum of well-being endowed my hopes with a semblance of truth. When before Christmas I wrote:

I have planted about fifteen rose stems which are now 12 rose bushes on the rise. 40 small pink roses were given to us last week. I planted an orange tree yesterday and five Trinitarias (Pride of Barbados), a beautiful climbing shrub/tree which flowers all year. 2 elderberry branches that are now little trees. Jasmine and all sorts.

It was true. What I didn't say was that for every rose stem that took, some thirty must have been dug up by the dogs and thrown away. Planting anything was the triumph of hope over experience. The orange tree was barricaded inside its own picket fence. The trinitarias were bunkered under barbed wire and the most noticeable aspect of the garden was a jungle of weeds. The child I was carrying was something else I could share with Joanne and did.

Be thinking, and let me know of girls' names that you like. I have found a lovely one: Iseult—ancient Irish. I'm not quite sure how to pronounce it. For a boy we have Alexander and Balthazar either or both.

Jaime and I had discussed children's names in Italy and I knew that Alexander or Balthazar was a mutual choice. I didn't mention that now that a baby was finally due, in the first week of April, it too had become a non-subject. Only when Jaime arrived on the hacienda with one of his innumerable cousins did my domestic life assume what might be described as normality. Since these were rare occasions, I came to prefer my solitude. There was something surreal about slipping in and out of the role of wife merely for the sake of an audience.

LISA ST. AUBIN DE TERÁN (1953–)
*The Hacienda: My Venezuelan Years*

# *Bleeding Hearts*

· · ·

KARL AND HIS father hired herders for the summer, and they all slept in tents in bachelor's bliss on the mountainside, watching sheep, watching for bears, trading stories with the look-out men who watched for forest fires from their lonely cabins. It was Karl who cooked for them, for the most part; he sometimes traded jobs with Pete and brought the horse down for supplies, as it gave him the chance to see Augusta. Later in the summer, lambs fat on alpine grasses were cut from the flock using a corral-and-chute system set up on the mountain, and they'd be driven, on foot, down to the nearest trail stockyards. From Queest Mountain, the lambs went to Malakwa to load; from Hunters Range they went to Salmon Arm. Once loaded onto stock cars, they were shipped to the Vancouver yards and from there to slaughterhouses.

Most of the time Augusta stayed behind, alone, on the Whorehouse Ranch. The summers were her quiet time, without Olaf or his wretched dog. She sat and drank coffee whenever she wanted, which was almost every morning. But she worked too: feeding and milking the cow, and feeding the pigs if they had them. The rest of her day was spent in her garden: tilling, planting, weeding, harvesting, and canning. They would depend on that produce through the winter. But tending these crops was no chore for Augusta; here in the garden, her senses tingled. She went barefoot, ate sweet strawberries warm off the plant, and dug her fingers into soil, into living earth. If she didn't own the house she kept, at least she could call this bit of land her own. She had bought it with sweat, invested in it with care. Her soul bloomed here with the flowers, and the smell of tomato plants and lavender quieted her. Here she was at rest.

The only flowers in the garden on her arrival were ratty weeds blooming insolently in the vegetable plot over the heads of carrots, potato plants, and cabbage so infested with cabbage moth that it looked as though some angry soul had peppered it with buckshot. She dug into the dry sandy soil around the house and made rectangular beds with two-by-fours, and brought in wheelbarrow after wheelbarrow of sheep manure to fill them. Planting a flower garden on her arrival at the end of August was a risky thing to do, because it was only with luck that the weather held long enough for her to get a few velvety snapdragons, a scattering of stubborn petunias, and a patch of hardy shasta daisies that sprang up triumphantly, rooting themselves there to bloom for years after.

Olaf couldn't see the sense in it. "Flowers aren't good for anything," he said. He was wrong. The garden filled her, extended her, made her more than she was without it. There was so little in that bachelor's cabin that she could call her own. The garden was her place, and she filled it with prettiness: lilac bushes cultured from saplings given to her by Mrs. Grafton, tulip, daffodil, and iris bulbs that she'd brought from home, and in the shade around the back of the house, bleeding hearts split from her mother's plant.

GAIL ANDERSON-DARGATZ (1963–)

*A Recipe for Bees*

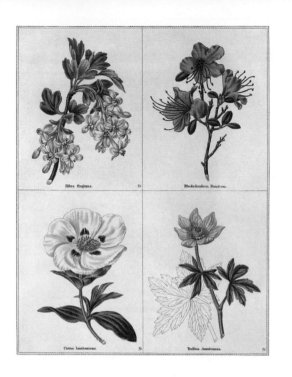

Ribes fragrans.

Rhododendron Dauricum.

Cistus lusitanicus.

Trollius Americanus.

Iris xanthospina.

Digitalis ambigua.

Clematis montana.

Echinacea dubia.

Tropaeolum peregrinum.

Gladiolus Colvillii.

Hedysarum Caucasicum.

Bulbine asphodeloides.

Pentstemon barbatum.

Scutellaria Japonica.

Leucelia Modecanea.

Erica Macbayana.

# Starting Over

· · ·

I DIDN'T PLANT my snap peas this year. I'm moving to Long Island—to a warmer, sandier soil—and someone else will be tilling my old plot in Ipswich, Massachusetts.

It's a beautiful site for a garden, a fifty-foot square in the middle of a wild meadow. It basks in full sunlight on the top of a knoll overlooking the confluence of the Ipswich River and a saltwater creek. At low tide, I can lean on my shovel and watch the clam diggers and the great blue herons; at high tide, the more frivolous boaters, speeding down the channel like Toady and Rat.

Leaving a piece of land is not an easy departure. Each place holds so many experiences—successes and failures with plants, bugs and people—that a move can't help feeling like some kind of erasure.

My husband and I first hacked at the matted field with borrowed pickaxes, ripping up the sod with our hands and shaking the topsoil from every piece back into the little square we had bounded by twine. He, a suburban kid, thought a small plot was plenty; I, a farmer's daughter, wanted half the field—for squash, potatoes and corn.

Months before, we'd argued over the seed catalogs. Why couldn't I be satisfied with a tidy little list, he grumbled. That was just like me, always wanting too much. Why couldn't I plant corn if I wanted, I complained. That was just like him, always trying to control me. You want to do everything *your way*, we both yelled, like furious adolescents.

Neither of us had learned the art of compromise, and as we went down the rows planting the beans and putting in the tomatoes, our boundaries solidified into rock walls, instead of blending in a comfortable combination of desires and tastes. When a pound of Burpee's Early Sunglow arrived in the mail—I'd willfully, secretly added it to the list—my husband turned on our big color TV and began rooting for the Red Sox. After all, maybe his favorite vegetation was the bright green outfield of Fenway Park.

The next April, I knelt in the cold damp earth, putting in as many peas as I wanted. My husband and I had given up gardening together—and on each other. The first little green shoots comforted me, in their sturdy urgency to get on with life, but the irony of my huge plot, for just me, was a bitter one. Who was going to eat all those vegetables that would fill the hefty Sears freezer my father had bought for us?

I began to grow flowers that summer. I realized why my father puttered in his rose beds, his own heart opening up as the hybrid teas and grandifloras bloomed. And by the time other men ventured into my garden, I knew enough to hand them the packet of Kentucky Wonder seeds and say, with a nonchalant shrug, "Plant them however you want, that's part of the fun." Sure, I was gritting my teeth, but I wanted to eat those beans across from a warm body.

Yet that little seaside plot also gave me clarity, helped me to trust my instincts. I longed for rhubarb, raspberries and asparagus, but I couldn't bring myself to put in any of these perennials with any of my gardening guests.

Perhaps I needed to do it all my own way for a while. I'd grown up with a man who'd welcomed his children in the vegetable plot—as long as we set the tomatoes out with military precision. No wonder my own garden grew in crooked rows and irregular patches, a slightly sloppy riot of vegetables and flowers. A kind of happy manifestation of my mind, which is more circular than linear.

But last summer, some blight seemed to pass through my healthy plot. The soil wasn't the problem; it had grown rich with years of compost and my neighbor's cow manure. It wasn't ignorance; I knew how to combat every bug and fungus. No, some malaise of my own had crept up to that seaside garden. When the Japanese beetles arrived, I failed to pick them off the bush beans in the evenings. I no longer stood patiently with the hose, letting my thirsty tomatoes drink their fill. Days would pass, and I'd stay away—playing with friends or reading wintry books inside the house—and when I did climb to the top of my little knoll, I'd find weeds choking my cucumbers, spider mites smothering my Brussels sprouts. It was no longer a happy experience to grow all this stuff alone. My little paradise had become a Garden of Neglect.

And so last fall, as I brought in the green tomatoes, and cut off the dropping heads of my Mammoth sunflowers, I knew that the spring would send me out into some new territory. I don't know what my new garden will be like. Some small suburban plot, set right against my neighbor's private hedge? Or a more private place, tucked behind the cottage on some wealthy old estate?

I'll miss the sea, and the herons, and the deer stepping delicately out into the meadow as the sun goes down. But I know that my next garden will put down longer, woodier roots. I find myself reading up on those asparagus beds. I'm studying the art of orchards. And I want my own grape arbor—to make enough wine for two.

ANNE RAVER (1949–)

*Deep in the Green*

# Shingle

. . .

*British filmmaker Derek Jarman started his garden*
*at a cottage in Dungeness, on the south coast of Kent, in view of*
*a nuclear power plant. He died later in the year he writes about*
*at the end of this excerpt of an* AIDS-*related illness.*

WHEN I CAME to Dungeness in the mid-eighties, I had no thought of building a garden. It looked impossible: shingle with no soil supported a sparse vegetation. Outside the front door a bed had been built—a rockery of broken bricks and concrete: it fitted in well. One day, walking on the beach at low tide, I noticed a magnificent flint. I brought it back and pulled out one of the bricks. Soon I had replaced all the rubble with flints. They were hard to find, but after a storm a few more would appear. The bed looked great, like dragon's teeth—white and grey. My journey to the sea each morning had purpose.

I decided to stop there; after all, the bleakness of Prospect Cottage was what had made me fall in love with it. At the back I planted a dog rose. Then I found a curious piece of driftwood and used this, and one of the necklaces of holey stones that I hung on the wall, to stake the rose. The garden had begun.

I saw it as a therapy and a pharmacopoeia. I collected more driftwood and stones and put them in. I dug small holes—almost impossible, as the shingle rolled back so that two spadefuls became one—and filled them with manure from the farm up the road. The plants were just plonked in and left to take their chances in the winds of Dungeness. The easterlies are the worst; they bring salt spray which burns everything. The westerlies only give a battering. We have the strongest sunlight, the lowest rainfall, and two less weeks of frost than the rest of the U.K. Dungeness is set apart, at "the fifth quarter," the end of the globe; it is the largest shingle formation, with Cape Canaveral, in the world . . .

At first, people thought I was building a garden for magical purposes—a white witch out to get the nuclear power station. It did have magic—the magic of surprise, the treasure hunt. A garden *is* a treasure hunt, the plants the paperchase.

I invest my stones with the power of those at Avebury. I have read all the mystical books about ley-lines and circles—I built the circles with this behind my mind. The circles make the garden perfect—in winter they take over from the flowers. There was magic and hard work in finding the coloured stones for the front: white, difficult; grey, less; red, very rare.

Some of the flints are over a foot high: these are the central hub; some are grey, a very few white and a warm brown, the others mottled white and grey. The bricks, washed smooth by the tide, bring a jolly flash of red. The large circles are four feet in diameter and between the flint dolmens are shells and coloured stones from the beach. The stakes are head-high. I haven't named them, so they are difficult to identify; some have the holey stones made into necklaces, some have large single stones or bone caps; there's one twisted tangle of chain

that has a lobster claw—that one *has* got a name: 'the snake'; there are wind chimes, two of them with metal triangles to ring. There is a lantern, a crucifix and a verdigris trumpet...

May 2: Bart's let me off the drip and Howard and I took off to Dungeness. The day was grey when we set out; we drove down the lanes in the shimmering green of May. Time brings a uniformity to

Fructus Artiſochi.

the spectrum of green. Along the verges of the lane are white ramsons, purple orchid, buttercup and bluebell. Up hill, down dale we go to Prospect Cottage, which grows like a tree—more beautiful the older it becomes. The garden is fresh and green as the lanes; it is filled with the flowers of spring: some wonderful tulips: crimson and yellow with a frill, and a deep purple one which sways above the luxuriant tawny wallflowers, the first white campion, blue-eyed forget-me-nots and banks of marigolds; the *Crambe cordifolia* and *maritima* are in bud, as are the Mrs. Sinkins pinks. The dragon-toothed rocks have almost disappeared, the garden is off, the gun of spring fired. The artichoke outside my window has fourteen buds and is shoulder high, the huge thistles have filled out, the roses are all in leaf, the sages are in bud, the everlasting peas sprawl around lazily across the shingle. The gorse, which took a battering, is sprouting.

The garden is therapeutic in its peacefulness. Howard Phostrogened and planted the herbs we bought in Iden Croft Herbs: low-growing thyme, tarragon, some pinks. We rooted out some double anemones—a flower destroyed by meddling—and put in a wine-black peony, and species elder and fennel around the cesspit.

At the side of the house the wooden sleeper squares looked magnificent, filled with shingle. Peter is still cutting the poem 'Busie old foole, unruly Sunne' for the side of the house. I'm going to ask them to carry on here and build two *Crambe* squares and freshen the stones in the beds. I returned to Bart's happy, all my little tasks fulfilled.

DEREK JARMAN (1942–94)
*Derek Jarman's Garden*

## STATEMENTS
## AND STYLE

ᴀʟʟ ɢᴀʀᴅᴇɴꜱ make statements about the way their owners see the world, but some are used expressly for that purpose. The wealthy spare no expense in decorating huge areas with exotic foliage and imposing buildings. Like art collectors, they invite dignitaries, friends, and subjects into their gardens to admire the beauty their money has created. Sultan Mehmet ɪɪ, who conquered Constantinople in 1453, employed 920 gardeners to keep his gardens at Topkapi Palace in shape. His head gardener also had to steer the sultan's barge (which was rowed by gardeners) and act as executioner.

< Turkish gardens of the Ottoman Empire
were filled with music, feasting, and poetry.

Those who can afford it may be avid followers of garden fashion, giving their gardens extensive makeovers when fashions change. In eighteenth-century England, the famed garden designer Lancelot "Capability" Brown swept away the knots and parterres of Elizabethan gardens in favor of artfully placed clumps of trees, lakes, and the undulating features of parkland. Humphry Repton came along with his Red Books, offering decorative detail to challenge Brown's ideal of wide-open spaces. European followers of the Picturesque called for thundering waterfalls, craggy rocks, and hermitages tucked into far-flung corners of an estate; the Romantics lauded Nature above all else; those with an adventurous turn of mind embraced chinoiserie. As trends ebbed and flowed, the art of clipping evergreens into complicated shapes was lauded, then reviled.

Beyond changing fashions, gardens reveal cultural attitudes. In Japan, each season has its treasure to offer the patient garden observer: the opening of the first plum blossom in spring, the fire of maples in the fall. For well-educated civil servants in China, gardens were spaces set aside for artistic and intellectual activity, and the garden was not considered complete until poetic descriptions of views and aspects had been included to enhance the visitor's experience.

In both China and Japan, a traditional garden was much like a landscape painting, capturing the artistic essence of Nature. This was a sentiment with which followers of the Picturesque movement in the late eighteenth century wholeheartedly agreed. At the end of the nineteenth century, the Arts and Crafts movement in England followed up on the idea of the garden as painting when Gertrude Jekyll planted her perennial beds in swathes of color like an artist applying paint to a canvas.

Garden owners may use their gardens to make pointed political statements or to comment on the world in which they live. Following the lead of Renaissance gardeners in Italy, European gentry laid out a trail of classical statuary to tell stories of heroism and glory to visitors who strolled around their estates. William Shenstone, in the mid-eighteenth century, meant his garden, The Leasowes, to be experienced in a particular order and became extremely vexed with visitors who chose not to follow his prescribed route. Contemporary poet and philosopher Ian Hamilton Finlay sees the garden as "an ideal and radical space, a space of mind beyond sight and touch." In his garden Little Sparta, he explores the relationship between Nature and Culture, "ambushing" the visitor at every turn with benches, headstones, and obelisks inscribed with language and juxtaposing classical heroes with the artifacts of modern warfare. Gardens such as Little Sparta and American Martha Schwartz's Splice Garden—an assemblage of fake boxwood, green gravel, paint, and Astroturf created in 1986 for a microbiology research center in Cambridge, Massachusetts—are intended to provoke debate.

## Mughal Splendor

· · ·

*Babur, a Muslim conqueror from Central Asia,*
*established the foundation for the Mughal Empire in India.*
*Shah Jahan, one of his successors, built the Taj Mahal.*

WHEN THE ALMIGHTY Disposer of events thought fit in his wisdom to confer the empire of Hindustaun upon our illustrious race, my ancestor the Emperor Baber... evinced his predilection for Agrah, by forming, on a spot on the opposite side of the Jumnah remarkable for the purity of the air, a spacious and magnificent garden. In one part of the garden he erected an elegant pavilion of hewn stone (green marble) of four stories, surmounted by a dome of twenty guzz [37 feet] in diameter, and surrounded by a colonnade or gallery, the pillars of which were of polished marble, and the ceilings decorated with gold and lapis-lazuli, formed into beautiful figures of the most elaborate workmanship. Within the gardens, moreover, he planted a covered avenue, carried to the distance of two kosse in length, all of sapaury trees, each of which grows to the height of fifty cubits [92 feet], the branches spreading at the top like an umbrella. In effect, for the formation of such an avenue, nothing can be better calculated than these lofty and graceful trees. In the centre of the garden (it might indeed without impropriety be called a park) lie formed a basin one kosse in circumference, the sides of which were faced all round with hewn stone, and in the centre of the basin he erected another pavilion of two stories, in which might be seated two hundred persons if necessary. The doors and walls of this also were decorated with beautiful figures of the most delicate designs, and the pavilion was approached by a convenient arched bridge of hewn stone. This garden extended altogether over a space of two hundred and fifty jerreibs [acres], and received the name of Bezugh-e-gulaf-shaun—the rose-diffusing. In an angle of the garden he also erected a spacious mosque, with a vaulted well attached... During the reign of the same illustrious monarch, many kinds of fruit foreign to the climate of Hindustaun were also introduced and planted in this garden. I shall mention one in particular, the ananauss (pine-apple), being among the most

delicious of those reared in the island of the Frengueis (or Portuguese); of which fruit this same garden has been known in a season to have produced nearly one hundred thousand.

Of other fruits which it produced in sufficient abundance, there were grapes of the most esteemed and delicious kinds, several kinds of apples, apricots of Suliman and Abbas, and beh-alu (some kind of plum), together with a variety of other sorts of fruits brought from Kabul and the parts of the west, hitherto strangers to the climate of Hindustaun, but now cultivated with abundant success. Here also was introduced the sandal tree, peculiar to the islands of Zeir, or Zubberbad. With regard to the Hindustauny fruits, they were in such multiplied variety as it would be tedious to enumerate. Of flowers there was every sort of the rose, and particularly the musk and damask rose, together with the jessamin and gultchemeily, the latter the most esteemed of Indian flowers. In short, the flowers and flowering shrubs introduced into the Gulafshaun garden were in such endless variety as to surpass all powers of description.

JAHANGIR (1569–1627)

*Memoirs of the Emperor Jahangueir*

# A Scholar's Haven

. . .

ALTHOUGH MY ROOMS are lowly and lack ornament, and my run-down kiosks are untiled, the scenic atmosphere is simple and rustic, as if set among cliffs and valleys. This can be admired.

In the garden is a hall of three bays. At its side are wings for housing my family. To the south of this is another hall, also of three bays. I call it Penetrating the Classics. This is where I discuss the Six Arts. To the east of the Hall for Penetrating the Classics is also the Milin Granary for storing the year's savings. There is a Crane Chamber for raising cranes and the Studio of Childish Innocence for instructing my children. At the northwest corner of the Hall for Penetrating the Classics is a high slope that I named Viewing Mountains Slope. On the slope is the Qin Terrace, and at the western corner there is the Studio for Chanting. These are the places where I strum my *qin* and compose poems, hence the names. Beneath the Seeing Mountains Slope is a pool... [In its center] is a kiosk called Ink Pool. Here I have gathered the masterpieces of the hundred masters [of calligraphy] and unroll them for my pleasure. On the bank of the pool is a pavilion called Brush Stream. I use its pure [water] to moisten my brush...

As to [my life] in this garden, in the morning I read aloud from *The Book of Changes* of Fuxi and King Wen, and *The Spring and Autumn Annals* of Confucius. I search out the subtle points of *The Book of Songs* and *The Book of History,* and clarify the systems and rules of *The Rites* and *Music.* In the evenings I inspect the myriad histories, and go in succession through the hundred masters. I research what

was right and wrong of ancient men, and rectify the accurate and inaccurate points in the former histories.

When I am at leisure, I roam about with my staff, climb heights and lean over depths. Flying birds are not frightened, and white cranes lead the way. I wade through the shallow flows, wander about level places. I plant trees and water the garden; in winter I plow, in summer I weed...

Although this garden was left to me by my late father, I have given my utmost to it for a very long time... A thousand years from now, people of Wu still will point to this place and say to one another, "This is the former garden of the Zhu family."

ZHU CHANGWEN, 1081

*"The Record of the Joy Garden"*

# Seasonal Debates

. . .

THE NEW ROKUJO mansion was finished in the Eighth Month and people began moving in. The southwest quarter, including her mother's lands, was assigned to [Empress] Akikonomu as her home away from the palace. The northeast quarter was assigned to the lady of the orange blossoms, who had occupied the east lodge at Nijo, and the northwest quarter to the lady from Akashi. The wishes of the ladies themselves were consulted in designing the new gardens, a most pleasant arrangement of lakes and hills.

The hills were high in the southeast quarter, where spring-blossoming trees and bushes were planted in large numbers. The lake was most ingeniously designed. Among the plantings in the forward parts of the garden were cinquefoil pines, maples, cherries, wisteria, yamabuki, and rock azalea, most of them trees and shrubs whose season was spring. Touches of autumn too were scattered through the groves.

In Akikonomu's garden the plantings, on hills left from the old garden, were chosen for rich autumn colors. Clear spring water went singing off into the distance, over rocks designed to enhance the music. There was a waterfall, and the whole expanse was like an autumn moor . . .

The Ninth Month came and Akikonomu's garden was resplendent with autumn colors. On an evening when a gentle wind was blowing she arranged leaves and flowers on the lid of an ornamental box and sent them over to Murasaki [in the spring garden]. Her messenger was a rather tall girl in a singlet of deep purple, a robe of lilac lined with blue, and a gossamer cloak of saffron. She made her practiced way along galleries and verandas and over the soaring bridges that joined them, with the dignity that became her estate, and yet so pretty that the eyes of the whole house were upon her. Everything about her announced that she had been trained to the highest service.

This was Akikonomu's poem, presented with the gift:

"Your garden quietly awaits the spring.

Permit the winds to bring a touch of autumn."

The praise which Murasaki's women showered on the messenger did not at all displease her. Murasaki sent back an arrangement of moss on the same box, with a cinquefoil pine against stones suggesting cliffs. A poem was tied to a branch of the pine:

"Fleeting, your leaves that scatter in the wind.

The pine at the cliffs is forever green with the spring."

One had to look carefully to see that the pine was a clever fabrication. Akikonomu was much impressed that so ingenious a response should have come so quickly. Her women were speechless.

"I think you were unnecessarily tart," said Genji to Murasaki. "You should wait until your spring trees are in bloom. What will the goddess of Tatsuta think when she hears you belittling the best of autumn colors? Reply from strength, when you have the force of your spring blossoms to support you.". . .

It was late in the Third Month. Murasaki's spring garden was coming ever more to life with blossoms and singing birds. . .

Japanese gardens highlight the transient nature of seasonal colors and textures.

Akikonomu was in residence at Rokujo. Now was the time, thought Murasaki, for a proper answer to the poem about the garden that "awaits the spring." Genji agreed. It would have been good to show these spring blossoms to the empress herself, but casual visits were out of the question for one in her position. Numbers of her young women who were thought likely to enjoy such an outing were therefore rowed out over the south lake, which ran from her southwest quarter to Murasaki's southeast, with a hillock separating the two. The boats left from the hillock. Murasaki's women were stationed in the angling pavilion at the boundary between the two quarters.

The dragon and phoenix boats were brilliantly decorated in the Chinese fashion. The little pages and helmsmen, their hair still bound up in the page-boy manner, wore lively Chinese dress, and everything about the arrangements was deliciously exotic, to add to the novelty, for the empress's women, of this southeast quarter. The boats pulled up below a cliff at an island cove, where the smallest of the hanging rocks was like a detail of a painting. The branches caught in mists from either side were like a tapestry, and far away in Murasaki's private gardens a willow trailed its branches in a deepening green and the cherry blossoms were rich and sensuous. In other places they had fallen, but here they were still at their smiling best, and along the galleries wisteria was beginning to send forth its lavender. Yellow *yamabuki* reflected on the lake as if about to join its own image. Waterfowl swam past in amiable pairs, and flew in and out with twigs in their bills, and one longed to paint the mandarin ducks as they coursed about on the water...

Today there was to be a reading of the Prajnaparamita Sutra commissioned by Empress Akikonomu... Murasaki had prepared the floral offerings. She chose eight of her prettiest little girls to deliver them, dressing four as birds and four as butterflies. The birds brought cherry blossoms in silver vases, the butterflies *yamabuki* in gold vases. In wonderfully rich and full bloom, they completed a perfect picture. As the party rowed out from the hillock to Akikonomu's end of the lake, a breeze came up to scatter a few cherry petals. The skies were clear and happy, and the little girls were charming in the delicate spring haze. Akikonomu had declined Murasaki's offer of awnings and had instead put out seats for the orchestra in one of the galleries adjoining her main hall. The little girls came to the stairs with their flowers. Incense bearers received them and set them out before the holy images.

Yugiri delivered this poem from Murasaki:

"Low in your grasses the cricket awaits the autumn

And views with scorn these silly butterflies."

Akikonomu smiled, recognizing an answer to her poem about the autumn leaves.

MURASAKI SHIKIBU (CA. 973–CA. 1014)

*Tale of Genji*

· · ·

IN THE GREAT View Garden there is a test of skill in composing inscriptions for the sides and over the doors...

Chia Chêng... thought deeply for a while and said: "These inscriptions are a difficult matter. Strictly speaking, we ought to invite the Imperial Concubine to give us the themes. But if the Imperial Concubine does not view the scenery for herself it will be difficult for her to come to a decision. If we wait until the Imperial Concubine makes her Imperial Progress and then ask for the themes, then all this scenery, all these pavilions and kiosques without a single word to exhibit a theme—granted that there are flowers, willows, hills, and water, there will be no beauty whatever about it."

The young gentlemen at his side all smiled and answered: "Venerable Sir, what you observe is perfectly true. Now we have an idea. A tablet and couplet for each place are certainly necessary and they certainly cannot be decided on. Now according to the scenery let whether two or three or four words according to their meaning in general be decided upon. And for the time being make lanterns and hang them up with these inscriptions on them to await the time of the Imperial Concubine's Progress. And then invite her to fix the names. Is not that a perfect arrangement for both parties?"...

The young gentlemen said: "And there is no difficulty about that. When we have all seen what the general idea is, let us each propose what he thinks the best. The excellent ones we will retain. The inferior ones we will expunge. There will be no objection to that."

Chia Chêng said: "That proposal is quite right. And fortunately the weather is mild today. Let us all go and have a stroll around."

So saying, he got up and led them all thither, Chia Chên going first into the Garden to give notice that they were coming...

Just when they had arrived at the Garden gate, [Pao-yü] saw Chia Chên at the head of a great number of men in charge of the work standing in attendance at the side.

Chia Chêng said: "You shut the Garden gate. We will first have a look outside and then we will go in."

Chia Chên gave orders for the gate to be shut. Chia Chêng first, standing straight in front of it, looked at the gate. He saw that the main gate had five gate-houses. On the top was a ridge of tubular tiles like a freshwater eel. The rails, the windows, the screens of the gate were all finely carved after the modern pattern. There was no red lime-wash ornamentation whatever; it was all smooth of one colour. At the base of all the walls were steps of white stone chiseled into the shape of the lotus of the far West. As one looked to the left and the right there were snow-white limewashed walls, at the base of which there were stones built up with lines like the stripes on the skin of a tiger. It did not fall into the vulgar style of rich ornamentation. Of course he was very pleased. He then commanded the gate to be opened and went in. Then they saw a range of bluish-green peaks blocking the way in front.

All the young gentlemen said: "What a fine hill! What a fine hill!"

Chia Chêng said: "If it were not for this one hill, as soon as one came in, all the scenery in the Garden would enter the eye. What pleasure would there be in that?"

They all said: "Quite so. Unless he had very beautiful scenery in his bosom how could he have thought of this?"

When they had finished speaking they went forward to have a look. They saw steep masses of white stone rising above one another, some like supernatural beings, some like fierce beasts, some upright, some stretched on the ground, some standing in a respectful attitude. On the top were mosses dotted about or wisteria, now out of sight and now in sight. In the midst could just be seen a little winding path.

Chia Chêng said: "Let us stroll along this little path. When we come back we will go out from that side. Then we shall have been able to see all over."

When he had finished speaking he ordered Chia Chên to lead the way. He himself was leaning on Pao-yü as they went in at the entrance to the hills by the winding path. Lifting up his head he suddenly saw a white rock like the face of a mirror on the hills. It was just the kind of place which meets the gaze and awaits a descriptive title.

Chia Chêng turned his head and said with a smile: "Gentlemen, please look. What would be the best name to give to this place?"

When they heard what he said, one of them said it could to be called "Range above range of bluish green," one of them said it ought to be called "Embroidered Peaks," one of them said "Sacrificial Incense Stove," one said "Miniature Chung-nan," all kinds of titles, more than several tens of them.

As a matter of fact all the guests already knew in their hearts that Chia Chêng wanted to put Pao-yü's ability to the test. That was why

< The Emperor Yang Ti (581–618) strolls
through his garden accompanied by his wives.

they only produced some conventional phrases for the sake of saying something. Pao-yü also knew that this was in their mind. Chia Chêng listened to them and then he turned his head and ordered Pau-yü to compose one.

Pao-yü said: "I have heard that the ancients said: 'To compose something new is not as good as to transmit something old. To carve something ancient is far better than to engrave something modern.' Moreover there is no presiding mountain or genuine scenery here. There is really nothing to be named. It is only a step forward to inspect the scenery. There is nothing better than to write above it that old word of the ancients: 'The winding path penetrates into the dark places.' That is a good prescription."

When they heard this they all praised it and said: "Quite right! Admirable! Second-generation elder brother's natural gifts are high, his ability is far-reaching, not like us who ought not to praise him too much"...

As he [Chia Chêng] was speaking they entered a rock cavern where they saw fine trees, marshy plants with reddish leaves and flowers, bulbous plants, and wonderful flowers all over the place, and a stream of clear running water issuing from the recesses among the flowers and trees under the cracks in the rock. Advancing a few steps further they came gradually towards the northern edge where it was level and open. On two sides towers stuck up high into the sky. Their carved roof-beams and ornamental railings were all hidden in the dips of the hills and the branches of the trees. When they looked down from above, all they could see were clear streams like flowing gems, stone steps going through the clouds, railings of white stone encircling pools and ponds, a stone bridge over three lagoons and animal faces spouting water. On the bridge was a pavilion.

When Chia Chêng and the others had come inside the pavilion and sat down, he asked: "What title do you gentlemen give to this?"

They all said: "In the 'Record of the Drunken Gentleman's Pavilion' of the duke of Ou-yang in former days it is said: 'There is a pavilion like wings.' Why not call it 'Wing-like'?"

Chia Chêng smiled and said, "Although 'Wing-like' is excellent, yet this pavilion has been built on water. It ought to have something to do with water in its name. According to my stupid decision, there is that expression of the duke of Ou-yang: 'Flowing between two peaks.' Use that word 'flowing' of his."

One of the guests said: "Quite right! Quite right! After all, the two words 'Flowing Gems' are excellent."

Chia Chêng stroked his beard and reflected. Then he told Pao-yü to decide again on a name.

Pao-yü replied: "What you have said just now, *Lao-yeh*, is right. But now if we investigate thoroughly it seems as if formerly, the duke of Ou-yang used the word 'Flowing' under the title 'The Wine Fountain'; and that was suitable. But now if we too use the word 'Flowing' because of this fountain, that seems to be unsatisfactory. Moreover since this place is a residence, separate from the family mansion, for the purpose of visiting parents, we ought to use a form which answers to this regulation. Also to use words of this kind seems very common and unrefined. I beg you to decide instead on something refined and reticent."

Chia Chêng smiled and said: "You have heard this gentleman. What is your opinion? Just now everybody composed a new name; you said it was not so good as to transmit something old. Now we transmit something old, and you say it is unsatisfactory because it is common. Now explain yours."

Pao-yü said: "If you use the two words 'Flowing Gems,' they are not as good as the two words 'Penetrating Fragrance.' Is not that fresh and elegant?"

Chia Chêng stroked his beard and nodded his head but said nothing. Everybody hastily welcomed it and agreed and praised Pao-yü's unusual talent.

Chia Chêng said: "Two words on a tablet are easy. Now compose a pair of antithetical scrolls each with seven words."

Pao-yü looked in every direction and set his mind to work. Then he recited:

"The willow trees on the encircling dyke lend three poles of green. The flowers on the opposite bank share in one strain of fragrance."
When Chia Chêng heard this he nodded his head and smiled.

CAO XUEQIN (CA. 1715–CA. 1763)

*Red Chamber Dream*

## *Gotta Have a Grotto*

. . .

YOU WILL INFINITLY oblige me: & give great encouragement to the worke I have in hand which is leveling my hill behind the house & making a Bowlin green; some Walkes & other devises, All [which?] my Cousen Evelyn directs; so that I hope it wilbe made very [word illegible], & render my seat very advantageous both for present & [future]. The bankes of my Walkes I would willingly set with some green Larell or the tree you mentioned, that it may looke green always: I intend to make upon my hill a very spatious Grotto & fountains below, my Water & ground being aprt for such things: if you can collect some curious shells or stones or pebbles: it will be very serviceable to me: in regard I mean to make it very Naturall: I will have the Water to come into it: & all along having my Cousen['s] advise I hope I shall doe nothing ill, a fault which formerly I have ben to guilty of.

GEORGE EVELYN

*Letter to his brother John, December 12, 1650*

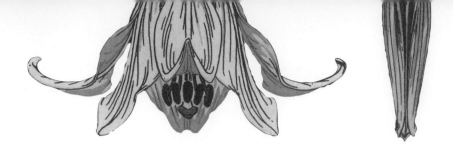

## Elizabethan Parterre

. . .

*This journal entry describes the garden at Hampton Court*
*in London as it was during the reign of Queen Elizabeth I.*

ON DESCENT AND exit from the church the gardener presented himself, and after we had offered a gratuity to our first guide, the gardener conducted us into the royal pleasaunce.

By the entrance I noticed numerous patches where square cavities had been scooped, as for paving stones; some of these were filled with red brickdust, some with white sand, and some with green lawn, very much resembling a chess-board. The hedges and surrounds were of hawthorn, bush firs, ivy, roses, juniper, holly, English or common elm, box and other shrubs, very gay and attractive.

There were all manner of shapes, men and women, half men and half horse, sirens, serving-maids with baskets, French lilies and delicate crenellations all round made from the dry twigs bound together and the aforesaid evergreen quick-set shrubs, or entirely of rosemary, all true to the life, and so cleverly and amusingly interwoven, mingled and grown together, trimmed and arranged picture-wise that their equal would be difficult to find.

THOMAS PLATTER THE YOUNGER (CA. 1574–1628)

# A Political Statement

. . .

*Sir Richard Temple used his garden at Stowe to comment
on the rotten state of government, going so far as to portray
the prime minister as a headless, armless statue.*

THE FIRST OF August we went to Stowe, which is beyond description. . . The buildings are indeed, in themselves, disagreeably crowded, but being dedicated to patriots, heroes, law-givers, and poets, and men of ingenuity and invention, they receive a dignity from the persons to whom they are consecrated. Others, that are sacred to imaginary powers, raise a pleasing enthusiasm in the mind.

What different ideas arise in a walk in Kensington gardens, or the Mall, where almost every other face wears impertinence! The great part of them unknown, and those with whom we are acquainted, only discover to us that they are idle, foolish, vain and proud. At Stowe you walk amidst heroes and deities, powers and persons whom we have been taught to honour; who have embellished the world with arts or instructed it in science; defended their country and improved it.

The temples that pleased me most, for the design to which they were consecrated, were those to Ancient Virtue, to Friendship, to the Worthies, and to Liberty.

MRS. ELIZABETH MONTAGU (1718–1800)

*Letter, 1744*

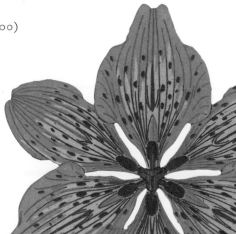

# Terrible Topiary

. . .

FOR THE BENEFIT of all my loving Country-men of this curious
Taste, I shall here publish a Catalogue of Green to be disposed of by
an eminent Town-Gardiner... Adam and Eve in Yew: Adam a little
shattered by the fall of the Tree of Knowledge in the great storm; Eve
and the serpent very flourishing.

The Tower of Babel, not yet finished.

St. George in Box; his arms scarce long enough, but will be in condition to stick the dragon by next April.

A green dragon of the same, with a tail of ground-ivy for the present.

N.B.—These two not to be sold separately.

Edward the Black Prince in cypress.

A laurustine bear in blossom, with a juniper hunter in berries.

A pair of giants, stunted, to be sold cheap.

A Queen Elizabeth in phylyraea, a little inclining to the green-
sickness, but full of growth.

Another Queen Elizabeth in myrtle, which was very forward, but
miscarried by being too near a Savine.

An old maid of honour in wormwood.

A topping Ben Jonson in laurel.

Divers eminent modern poets in bays, somewhat blighted, to be
disposed of, a pennyworth.

> Topiary at Levens Hall, Cumbria, England

A quickset hog, shot up into a porcupine, by its being forgot a week in rainy weather.

A lavender pig with sage growing in his belly.

Noah's ark in Holly standing on the mound; the ribs a little damaged for want of water.

ONE DAY THEIR walk led them down from the gate at the right wing of the castle, in the direction of the hotel, and thence over the bridge toward the ponds, along the sides of which they proceeded as far as it was generally thought possible to follow the water; thickly wooded hills sloped directly up from the edge, and beyond these a wall of steep rocks, making further progress difficult, if not impossible. But Edward, whose hunting experience had made him thoroughly familiar with the spot, pushed forward along an overgrown path with Ottilie, knowing well that the old mill could not be far off, which was somewhere in the middle of the rocks there. The path was so little frequented, that they soon lost it; and for a short time they were wandering among mossy stones and thickets; it was not for long, however, the noise of the water-wheel speedily telling them that the place which they were looking for was close at hand. Stepping forward on a point of rock, they saw the strange old, dark, wooden building in the hollow before them, quite shadowed over with precipitous crags and huge trees.

They determined directly to climb down amidst the moss and the blocks of stone. Edward led the way; and when he looked back and saw Ottilie following, stepping lightly, without fear or nervousness, from stone to stone, so beautifully balancing herself, he fancied he was looking at some celestial creature floating above him; while if, as she often did, she caught the hand which in some difficult spot he would offer her, or if she supported herself on his shoulder, then he was left in no doubt that it was a very exquisite human creature who touched him. He almost wished that she might slip or stumble, that he might catch her in his arms and press her to his heart. This, however, he would under no circumstances have done, for more than one reason. He was afraid to wound her, and he was afraid to do her some bodily injury...

Under the miller's guidance, Charlotte and the Captain came down by an easier path, and now joined them. There was the meeting, and a happy talk, and then they took some refreshments. They would not return by the same way as they came; and Edward struck into a rocky path on the other side of the stream, from which the ponds were again to be seen. They made their way along it, with some effort, and then had to cross a variety of wood and copse—getting glimpses, on the land side, of a number of villages and manor-houses, with their green lawns and fruit-gardens; while very near them, and sweetly situated on a rising ground, a farm lay in the middle of the wood. From a gentle ascent, they had a view, before and behind, which showed them the richness of the country to the greatest advantage; and then, entering a grove of trees, they found themselves, on again emerging from it, on the rock opposite the castle.

They came upon it rather unexpectedly, and were of course delighted. They had made the circuit of a little world; they were standing on the spot where the new building was to be erected, and were looking again at the windows of their home.

They went down to the summer-house, and sat all four in it for the first time together; nothing was more natural than that with one voice it should be proposed to have the way they had been that day, and which, as it was, had taken them much time and trouble, properly laid out and gravelled, so that people might loiter along it at their leisure. They each said what they thought; and they reckoned up that the circuit, over which they had taken many hours, might be traveled easily with a good road all the way round to the castle, in a single one.

Already a plan was being suggested for making the distance shorter, and adding a fresh beauty to the landscape, by throwing a bridge across the stream, below the mill, where it ran into the lake; when Charlotte brought their inventive imagination somewhat to a standstill, by putting them in mind of the expense which such an undertaking would involve.

JOHANN WOLFGANG VON GOETHE (1749–1832)
*Elective Affinities*

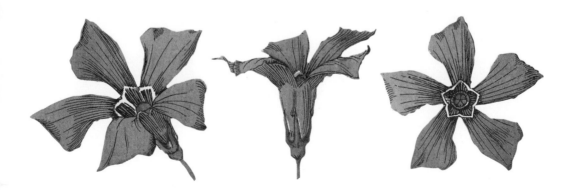

# Do-It-Yourself Design

· · ·

THEY FOUND IN their library the work by Boitard entitled *The Architect of the Garden.*

The author divides gardens into an infinity of styles. There is, in the first place, the Melancholy or Romantic, which is distinguished by everlastings, ruins, tombs, and an "ex-voto to the Virgin, indicating the spot where a cavalier has fallen under an assassin's dagger." The Terrible is constructed with overhanging rocks, shattered trees and burnt-out cabins; the Exotic by planting Peruvian torch-thistles "to bring back memories to a settler or traveler." The Pensive must provide, like Ermenonville, a temple to philosophy. Obelisks and triumphal arches characterise the Majestic; moss and grottoes, the Mysterious; a lake, the Poetic. There is even the Fantastic, of which the finest specimen was lately to be seen in Wurttemberg, for there one encountered successively a wild boar, a hermit, several tombs, and a boat which left the bank of its own accord, in order to convey the visitor to a drawing-room where jets of water drenched him as he lay down on the sofa.

In the face of this wonderland, Bouvard and Pécuchet experienced a kind of vertigo. The Fantastic seemed to them reserved for royalty. The temple to philosophy would be a cumbrance. The ex-voto to the Madonna would lack significance, seeing there were no assassins, and, so much the worse for the settlers and travelers, American plants were too expensive. But rocks were possible, as well as shattered trees, everlastings and moss; and with growing enthusiasm, after

much experiment, helped by a single handyman and for a trifling sum, they made for themselves a residence that was unparalleled in the whole district.

GUSTAVE FLAUBERT (1821–80)

*Bouvard and Pécuchet*

## The Formal Garden

### · · ·

I AM FRANKLY and absolutely for a formal garden. This may turn you away from me, but I hope not. Once and for all I declare against the thing called "landscape-gardening," and cleave to classic precedents. Note the high tone I take in this matter. With a house like mine there really is some excuse for seeking to ignore it, and developing a garden that shall be independent of architecture so dreadful; but no, I will be just; my garden shall shame my house by its correct proportions and proper adherence to what a garden ought to be. Not that this garden is classic—far from that; I wish it was. But it is a garden, no mere feeble deception. It is a small piece of ground enclosed by walls; and, concerning those walls, you are in no doubt for one moment. There is not the least attempt to imitate natural scenery. There are no winding walks, no boscages, no sylvan dells, no grottoes stuck with stones and stalactites. My garden is simply an artificial, but none the less beautiful, arrangement of all the best plants that I can contrive to collect.

Consider the word "garden." It develops by evolution from the Anglo-Saxon "geard" and the Middle English "garth." It means "a yard." It has rather less than nothing to do with wild nature, or any other sort of nature. It is a highly artificial contrivance within hard and fast boundaries. We speak of a zoological garden, a garden of pleasure, a garden of vegetables. To talk of a "natural" or a "wild" garden, is a contradiction in terms. You might as well talk of a natural "zoo," and do away with bars, and arrange bamboo brakes for the tigers, mountain-tops for the eagles, and an iceberg for the polar bears.

Pope and Addison began the "natural" theory, or fell in with it as soon as others set the fashion. They were about as intimate with nature as my chimney-sweep is with the latest Russian fiction; but it happened to be the cant of the time, and they reflected their hour and preached the return to Nature—*du sein des boudoirs*. Remember that very fine jest against our landscape-gardening: "Rien n'est plus facile que de dessiner un parc anglais; on n'a qu'à enivrer son jardinier, et à suivre son tracé." I scorn a park, or garden either, planned upon that groggy pattern. My paths are straight or circular, as the case requires: there is no meandering with me. You will perhaps answer sharply that one cannot meander in an acre, and that I am like the fox with his tail gone: I pretend to admire what I have no power to evade. Believe me, you are wrong. As I say elsewhere, if my garden were a thousand acres, it should sternly subscribe to form and design. The architect and the gardener, like "the walrus and the carpenter," should walk hand in hand; and I am very sure they would not weep, if I had the privilege to employ them upon a garden worthy of the name. Besides, you *can* meander in an acre. I have seen the most horrible tortuosities in half that space.

It is all very well for Addison to quote Horace and Virgil, and say that art is but the reflection of nature, and that natural things are more grand and august than any we may meet with amid the curiosities of art; but in the very midst of these platitudes he urges us to help and improve the natural embroidery of the meadows by small additions of art, and set off rows of hedges with trees and flowers. Landscape-gardening has produced a deal of fine writing, and been the death of the old severe instincts. In this place the result of these views about

nature is, that nine gardens out of ten are smothered with trees, and become mere natural factories of leaf-mould and nothing more. The houses are worthy of these gardens. The trees thrust their elbows in at the windows; then people talk about rheumatism. Give me light and air in a garden—even before plants.

---

With a little skill on the part of the gardener, a tree may be trained to useful service.

Upon this subject hear Mr. Reginald Blomfield, the world-famous architect, who is responsible for some of the most distinguished modern gardens in the United Kingdom. He is a hard hitter, I promise you, and speaks thus in his "Formal Garden of England"—a fascinating book that you ought not to be without. "The formal gardener is by his principles entitled to do what he likes with nature, but the landscapist gets involved in all sorts of contradictions. He 'copies nature's graceful touch,' but under totally different conditions to the original; so far, therefore, from being loyal to nature, he is engaged in a perpetual struggle to prove her an ass."

Now this sound argument justified me in planting yucca, agapanthus, and acacia, since I am a formal gardener, and my object is not to imitate nature but to exhibit her productions in a place specially ordered for that purpose; but the disciples of Mr. Robinson have no right to set up bananas in their glades, or foreign foliage plants for summer bedding. Their avowed ambition and aim is to copy nature as closely as they can; and nature does not grow the flora of Africa with that of Europe, or mingle the bog plants of North America and her productions from the Himalayas. To be logical, every non-indigenous plant should be banished from these "natural gardens." Push the precept to its just conclusion, and you arrive at a piece of wild waste land, which is the most perfect natural garden anybody can aspire to—in other words, not a garden at all.

EDEN PHILLPOTTS (1862–1960)

*My Garden*

# A Gardener's Palette

. . .

I AM STRONGLY of the opinion that the possession of a quantity of plants, however good the plants may be themselves and however ample their number, does not make a garden; it only makes a collection. Having got the plants, the great thing is to use them with careful selection and definite intention. Merely having them, or having them planted unassorted in garden spaces, is only like having a box of paints from the best colourman, or, to go one step further, it is like having portions of these paints set out upon a palette. This does not constitute a picture; and it seems to me that the duty we owe to our gardens and to our own bettering in our gardens is so to use the plants that they shall form beautiful pictures; and that, while delighting our eyes, they should be always training those eyes to a more exalted criticism; to a state of mind and artistic conscience that will not tolerate bad or careless combination or any sort of misuse of plants, but in which it becomes a point of honour to be always striving for the best. It is just in the way it is done that lies the whole difference between commonplace gardening and gardening that may rightly claim to rank as a fine art. Given the same space of ground and the same material, they may either be fashioned into a dream of beauty, a place of perfect rest and refreshment of mind and body—a series of soul-satisfying pictures— a treasure of well-set jewels; or they may be so misused that everything is jarring and displeasing. To learn how to perceive the difference and how to do right is to apprehend gardening as a fine art. In practice it is to place every plant or group of plants with such thoughtful care and definite intention that they shall form a part of a harmonious whole, and that successive portions, or in some cases even single details, shall show a series of pictures. It is so to regulate the trees and undergrowth of the wood that their lines and masses come into beautiful form and harmonious proportion; it is to be always watching, noting and doing, and putting oneself meanwhile into closest acquaintance and sympathy with the growing things. In this spirit, the garden and woodland, such as they are, have been formed. There have been many failures, but, every now and then, I am encouraged and rewarded by a certain measure of success. Yet, as the critical faculty becomes keener, so does the standard of aim rise higher; and, year by year, the desired point seems always to elude attainment. But, as I may perhaps have taken more trouble in working out certain problems, and given more thought to methods of arranging growing flowers, especially in ways of colour-combination, than amateurs in general, I have thought that it may be helpful to some of them to describe as well as I can by word, and to show by plan and picture, what I have tried to do, and to point out where I have succeeded and where I have failed.

GERTRUDE JEKYLL (1843–1932)

*Colour in the Flower Garden*

LADY CROOM. Your drawing is a very wonderful transformation. I would not have recognized my own garden but for your ingenious book—is it not?—look! Here is the Park as it appears to us now, and here as it might be when Mr. Noakes has done with it. Where there is the familiar pastoral refinement of any Englishman's garden, here is an eruption of gloomy forest and towering crag, of ruins where there was never a house, of water dashing against rocks where there was neither spring nor a stone I could not throw the length of a cricket pitch. My hyacinth dell is become a haunt for hobgoblins, my Chinese bridge, which I am assured is superior to the one at Kew, and for all I know at Peking, is usurped by a fallen obelisk overgrown with briars—

NOAKES *(bleating)*. Lord Little has one very similar—

LADY CROOM. I cannot relieve Lord Little's misfortunes by adding to my own. Pray, what is this rustic hovel that presumes to superpose itself on my gazebo?

NOAKES. That is the hermitage, madam.

LADY CROOM. The hermitage? I am bewildered.

BRICE. It is all irregular, Mr. Noakes.

NOAKES. It is, sir. Irregularity is one of the chiefest principles of the picturesque style—

LADY CROOM. But Sidley Park is already a picture, and a most amiable picture too. The slopes are green and gentle. The trees are

Temple de l'amour, Malmaison, France, 1893

companionably grouped at intervals to show them to advantage. The rill is a serpentine ribbon unwound from the lake peaceably contained by meadows on which the right amount of sheep are tastefully arranged—in short, it is nature as God intended, and I can say with the painter, "*Et in Arcadia ego!*" "Here I am in Arcadia," Thomasina.

THOMASINA. Yes, Mama, if you would have it so.

LADY CROOM. Is she correcting my taste or my translation?

TOM STOPPARD (1937–)

*Arcadia*

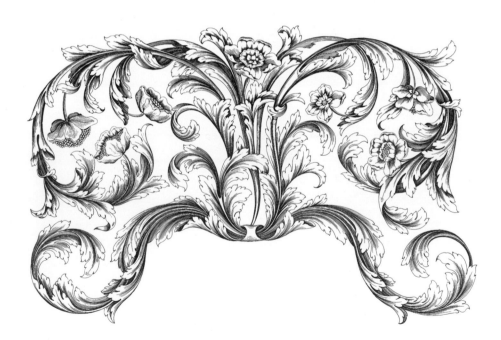

# Designed to Disturb

. . .

*Scottish gardener, sculptor, and poet Ian Hamilton Finlay created his own testament to the state of the world. At Little Sparta, he transformed the land around an abandoned croft near Dunsyre into a showcase of his intellectual investigations into human society.*

*Certain gardens are described as retreats when they are really attacks.*

IAN HAMILTON FINLAY

THE PARADOX—the unexpected challenge to assumptions and the revelation of death in the apparently simple—will be a recurring feature of the garden.

Deep in the Wild Garden, where the path leads on to the upper ponds, stand two imposing gate piers crowned by what seem, at a casual glance, to be classical urns or finials, but are hand grenades of the British Second World War design, often nicknamed "pineapples" because of their shape. They stand monumentally made from stone, their firing rings draping over their shoulders as ivy might over the expected finials; a characteristic conundrum whose elements are humour, beauty and threat.

A very different little wicket gate is set into the fence surrounding the Stonypath Allotment. Its simple inscription KAILYARD repeats the name given to the late-nineteenth-century group of Scottish writers such as J.M. Barrie and S.R. Crockett who treated the lives and concerns of Scots people in a sentimental way often unjustly scorned by critics. Kail, sometimes spelled kale, a particularly hardy kind of cabbage, was at one time a staple of the Scottish diet and its usurpation in contemporary life by more glamorously exotic foods is not likely to have done the Scots much good.

In an upland garden such as this it is appropriate to find stiles connecting the wilder hillsides with the tamer garden, and there are two connecting the upper pond garden with the moorland. A philosophical one has a triple inscription in the manner of Friedrich Hegel, whose idealism held reason to be the heart of reality. The proposition reads THESIS *fence* ANTITHESIS *gate,* then, as the farther side is reached, SYNTHESIS *stile.*

The adapted dictionary definition, a device Finlay uses frequently, underlines the poetic and literary nature of his work. The apparent precision and conciseness of a definition is brought to bear in ways which reveal unexpected aspects of the objects they describe and often dissolve the accepted meaning of terms, or interpretation of their reference in the 'real' world. The second stile carries such a definition of its physical and its ideal nature:

STILE *n. an escalation of the footpath*

JESSIE SHEELER, 2003

*Little Sparta*

## The Art of Setting Stones

. . .

THE GARDEN STONES are calming; their mute presence somehow reassuring. I sit on the veranda to be closer to them the way one will sit at the edge of the ocean, not needing to enter to be refreshed. The stones cast shadows, marking out dark crescents on the sand. They are brown, but not uniform in color—some rust, others coffee, all gnarled and angular. They have been set out in space to develop a tension, an imbalance that gives the garden its visual vitality, like the positioning of the mountains in an ink landscape, scattered about in the mist. Though many explanations have been attributed to [this temple] garden over the years, the meaning remains unclear. Still, an inherent understanding of the potency of imbalance applies, even as it does to the ink landscape paintings that served as models for the garden's design. The natural world has provided many symbols and motifs for artists—plum blossoms to express evanescence, running water to reveal nature's constant flux—but the landscape itself supplies the most compelling philosophy, a single, potent thought. Imbalance is energy. . .

When we look at something natural that pleases aesthetically—the pendulous curve of a branch, waves rolling at sea, this temple garden of only stones and sand—we find small-scale imbalances that animate it and make it dynamic and attractive. But at the same time we find the object expresses an inherent large-scale balance (it must if it is truly "natural") that we instinctively respond to, that puts us at ease, is somehow reassuring. Surely the beauty of this garden stems from the combination of the two: a delicate interplay of stillness and energy.

The imbalances that foster energy in nature, that power our societies and drive our economies, are distilled in this garden into just a few stones, held in tension across a field of raked white sand. And, like batteries that flow only when connected or space that is ascribed a value only when linked to those desirous of it, so the imbalance in the garden activates and begins to flow only when observed . . . by us. It is we, at the veranda's edge or in the shadows of the room nearby, who complete the link and turn the potential energy of the garden into reality, and to our delight we find the wellspring endless. We drink our fill in peace, steady in our faith it will not run dry. Unlike chemistry or economics, the energy of art is provided without loss to itself.

MARC PETER KEANE (1958–)

*The Art of Setting Stones*

< Ando Hiroshige, *Plum Estate, Kameido*, 1857

# The Garden of Cosmic Speculation

. . .

*Charles Jencks, the creator of the postmodernist garden described here, believes: "Nature is basically curved, warped, undulating, jagged, zigzagged, and sometimes beautifully crinkly. It never looks like a Platonic temple."*

THE DNA AND Physics Garden is altered and improved annually by Jencks, but the basic grid plan of its formal parterre is constant and based on the five human senses plus the sixth sense, the female sense of intuition or anticipation. Each area is centered around a sculptural version of the DNA double helix. *Sight* is perhaps the most dramatic of these. It contains a miniature version of the fifty-foot-high spiral mound in the shape of a double helix. Inside the mound is a grottolike room, with crinkly black and white fractal-banded wall patterns. At the top is an opening in the shape of an M. On bright days this casts the form of the letter inside the room, as a commemoration of Jencks's late wife, Maggie. *Smell* is represented by fragrant thyme plants that encircle the flared nostrils of a nose from which Jencks wants the smell of rotten vegetables to exude. *Hearing* is an ear trumpet finial that pivots in the wind activating chimes and bells. *Touch* is a sculpted hand rising above thistles and nettles, enclosed by a DNA double helix built of blocks. *Taste* has an aluminum mouth and thyme suspended above two species of wild strawberry. Finally, *Anticipation* is a woman looking at her open brain as it receives impulses from her fingers, which wave in the breeze—the sense of intuiting the future by picking up and interpreting vibrations.

GUY COOPER (1934–) AND GORDON TAYLOR (1935–)

*159*

*Gardens for the Future*

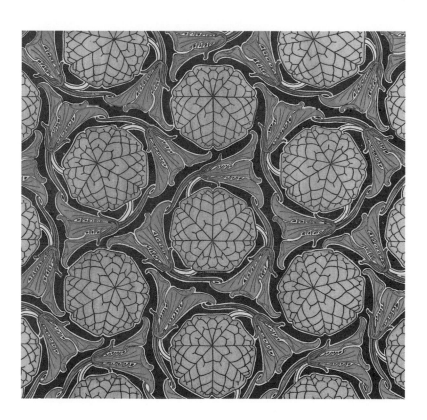

. . .

I ASKED A schoolboy, in the sweet summertide, "what he thought a garden was for?" and he said, *Strawberries*. His younger sister suggested *Croquet*, and the elder *Garden-parties*. The brother from Oxford made a prompt declaration in favour of *Lawn Tennis and Cigarettes*, but he was rebuked by a solemn senior, who wore spectacles, and more

*160*

black hair than is usual with males, and was told that "a garden was designed for botanical research, and for the classification of plants." He was about to demonstrate the differences between the *Acoty-* and the *Monocoty-ledonous* divisions, when the collegian remembered an engagement elsewhere.

I repeated my question to a middle-aged nymph, who wore a feath- ered hat of noble proportions over a loose green tunic with a silver belt, and she replied, with a rapturous disdain of the ignorance which presumed to ask—"What is a garden for? For the soul, sir, for the soul of the poet! For visions of the invisible, for grasping the intangible, for hearing the inaudible, for exaltations" (she raised her hands, and stood tiptoe, like jocund day upon the misty mountain top, as though she would soar into space) "above the miserable dullness of common life into the splendid regions of imagination and romance." I ventured to suggest that she would have to do a large amount of soaring before she met with anything more beautiful than the flowers, or sweeter than the nightingale's note; but the flighty one still wished to fly.

A capacious gentleman informed me that nothing in horticulture touched him so sensibly as green peas and new potatoes, and he spoke with so much cheerful candour that I could not be angry; but my indignation was roused by a morose millionaire, when he declared that of all his expenses he grudged most the outlay on his confounded garden.

S. REYNOLDS HOLE (1819–1904)

*Our Gardens*

# REFLECTIONS
# OF RANK

*G*ARDENS CAN be large or small, elaborate or simple. The form a garden takes often reflects the social circumstances of the garden owner. It is a time-honored tradition for the wealthy city family to maintain a weekend country retreat where important friends can be discreetly entertained. Whether off the beaten track or in town, the gardens of the wealthy are popular venues for extravagant entertainments. Ahmet III, sultan of the Ottoman Empire from 1703 to 1730, attached lights to tortoises and set them wandering through tulip beds

< This magnificent building combines a conservatory and an aviary.

to illuminate evening picnics. A moonlit garden strung with lights creates a world where alternate identities can be enjoyed.

The tall hedges, stone walls, and forbidding iron gates of large estates signal to those on the outside that privileged lives are being enjoyed within. But in the comfort of suburbia, middle-class families can relax in their gardens just as well. In England to this day, allotment gardening provides a rhythm to community life and a focal point for celebrating the partnership between hard work and natural abundance. Community gardens across North America reach out to urban, immigrant, and low-income families and encourage growers to donate fresh produce to local food banks, drawing those at the margins of society closer to its center.

People of all classes and backgrounds take enormous pride in their ability to coax horticultural wonders from the earth. Diana Balmori and Margaret Morton have documented the gardens of the homeless people in New York City. In The Hill, an area by Manhattan's Chinatown, residents jointly tend a garden of tomatoes, basil, peppers, and marigolds. The gardeners are not always sober, and fertilizer is manure salvaged from passing police horses. These gardeners sow a garden to change the way the world sees them and to change the way they see the world. The work gives them dignity; the beauty they coax from abandoned spaces gives them hope.

Those who move far from home often pack seeds and cuttings so they can plant gardens that will keep homesickness at bay. A community garden in New York City called Tranquilidad is a densely green space that conjures up the lushness of Puerto Rico. Less benign are the gardens of colonizing peoples that spill out into the surrounding culture, obliterating indigenous ideas of what it is to garden. As historical circumstances change, gardeners may abandon their gardens, but tough plants, once seeded, continue to reach for the sky.

MY HOUSE IS on the lower slopes of a hill but commands as good a view as if it were higher up, for the ground rises so gradually that the slope is imperceptible, and you find yourself at the top without noticing the climb. Behind it is the Apennine range, though some way off, so that even on a still and cloudless day there is a breeze from the mountains, but one which has had its force broken by the distance so that it is never cutting nor boisterous. It faces mainly south, and so from midday onwards in summer (a little earlier in winter) it seems to invite the sun into the colonnade. This is broad, and long in proportion, with several rooms opening out of it as well as the old-fashioned type of entrance hall.

In front of the colonnade is a terrace laid out with box hedges clipped into different shapes, from which a bank slopes down, also with figures of animals cut out of box facing each other on either side. On the level below there waves—or I might have said ripples—a bed of acanthus. All round is a path hedged by bushes which are trained and cut into different shapes, and then a drive, oval like a racecourse, inside which are various box figures and clipped dwarf shrubs. The whole garden is enclosed by a dry-stone wall which is hidden from sight by a box hedge planted in tiers; outside is a meadow, as well worth seeing for its natural beauty as the formal garden I have described; then fields and many more meadows and woods.

From the end of the colonnade projects a dining-room: through its folding doors it looks on to the end of the terrace, the adjacent meadow, and the stretch of open country beyond, while from its windows on one side can be seen part of the terrace and the projecting wing of the house, on the other the tree-tops in the enclosure of the adjoining riding-ground. Almost opposite the middle of the colonnade is a suite of rooms set slightly back and round a small court shaded by four plane trees. In the centre a fountain plays in a marble basin, watering the plane trees round it and the ground beneath them with a light spray. In this suite is a bedroom which no daylight, voice, nor sound can penetrate, and next to it an informal dining-room where I entertain my personal friends; it looks on to the small courtyard, the colonnade, and the view from the colonnade. There is also another room, green and shady from the nearest plane tree, which has walls decorated with marble up to the ceiling and a fresco (which is no less attractive) of birds perched on the branches of trees. Here is a small fountain with a bowl surrounded by tiny jets which together make a lovely murmuring sound. At the corner of the colonnade is a large bedroom facing the dining-room; some windows look out on to the terrace, others on to the meadow, while just below the windows in front is an ornamental pool, a pleasure both to see and to hear, with its water falling from a height and foaming white when it strikes the marble.

PLINY THE YOUNGER (CA. 61–CA. 113)

*Letter to Domitius Apollinaris*

# The Lady Throws a Party

· · ·

AS A CONSIDERABLE period had elapsed since I had an opportunity
of visiting the province of Gujerat, I felt a desire now I was in the
neighbourhood to view it in its present state, and I accordingly quitted
Mandou, after making the necessary preparations, and proceeded in
that direction. When my father had completed the subjugation of the
province, he had particularly enjoined every member of his court to
erect at different stations on the frontiers convenient buildings, with
gardens attached, and every requisite whether for repose or recreation.
Now when we approached the capital of the province, the first place
at which I encamped happened to be the villa and gardens of Khaun
Khanan, close to the suburbs of Ahmedabad. Kheyr-ul-Nessa Begum,
the daughter of that nobleman, who was present among the inmates
of my harram, now came to me, and stating her wish to entertain me
in these gardens of her father, requested that I would remain upon the
spot for a few days, while she expedited the necessary arrangements
for my reception. With a request which had its source in such motives
of kindness I could not refuse to comply, and I accordingly contin-
ued encamped in the neighbourhood. I must not omit to observe by
the way, that it was during that season of the year in which, from the
effects of the cold weather, most trees and shrubs usually shed their
foliage, and are equally bare of leaf, and fruit, and blossom.

In the course of five days, by employing various artificers of
Ahmedabad, to the number of four hundred individuals, in different

169

---

< A walled garden in Persia, circa 1450

branches of decoration, she had so effectually changed the appearance of the gardens, by making use of coloured paper and wax, that every tree and shrub seemed as abundantly furnished with leaf, and flower, and fruit, as if in the very freshness and bloom of spring and summer. These included the orange, lemon, peach, pomegranate, and apple; and among flowering shrubs, of every species of rose, and other garden flowers of every description. So perfect, indeed, was the deception produced, that when I first entered the garden it entirely escaped my recollection that it was no longer the spring of the year, nor the season for fruit, and I unwittingly began to pluck at the fruit and flowers, the artificers having copied the beauties of nature with such surprising truth and accuracy. You might have said, without contradiction, that it was the very fruit and flower you saw, in all its bloom and freshness. The different avenues throughout the garden were at the same time furnished with a variety of tents and canopies, of velvet of the deepest green; so that these, together with the verdure of the sod, contrasted with the variegated and lively tints of the rose and an infinity of other flowers, left altogether such an impression on my mind, as that in the very season of the rose I never contemplated in any place, garden, or otherwise, any thing that afforded equal delight to the senses.

From this scene of fascination and enchantment I was not permitted to withdraw myself for three days and as many nights; during which, independently of the delicious repasts on which we feasted, the females of my harram by whom I was accompanied, to the number of four hundred, were each of them presented with a tray of four pieces of

cloth of gold of the manufacture of Khoras-saun, and an ambertchei, or perfume-stand, of elaborate workmanship and considerable value; none of which presents could have been estimated separately at a less sum than three hundred tomauns. What the begum presented to myself on the occasion, in jewels, pieces of the richest fabric for my wardrobe, and horses of the highest value for temper and speed, could not have amounted to a less sum than four laks of rupees. In return, I presented her with a chaplet of pearl of the value of five laks of rupees, which had been purchased for my own use, and a bulse of rubies worth three laks more: I also added one thousand horse to the dignity already possessed by her father. In conclusion, what was thus exhibited in one short week, and in the very depth of winter, for my recreation, by the daughter of Khaun Khanan alone, could scarcely have been accomplished by the united genius and skill of any hundred individuals of the other sex, chuse them where you may.

JAHANGIR (1569–1627)

*Memoirs of the Emperor Jahangueir*

· · ·

1 LEAVING THE Château by the vestibule of the marble courtyard, go onto the terrace. You must stop at the top of the steps to consider the arrangement of the parterres, the pools and the fountains in the Cabinets.

2 Next you must go directly above Latona, and pause to consider Latona, the lizards, the flight of steps, the statues, the Royal Allée, Apollo, the Canal, and then turn round to see the parterres and the Château.

3 Then you must turn left to proceed between the Sphinxes. While walking, you must pause before the Cabinet to consider the tall jet and the sheet of water. Reaching the Sphinxes, pause to see the South Parterre, and then go directly above the Orangery, where you will see the parterre of the orange-trees and the Lake of the Swiss Guards.

4 Turn right, and proceed up between the statues of Apollo in bronze and Antonius; pause at the limit of the terrace where you see Bacchus and Saturn.

5 Go down the flight of steps to the right of the Orangery, and proceed into the garden of the orange-trees. Go straight to the fountain, and there consider the Orangery. Proceed along the allées of large orange-trees, then into the covered orangery, leaving it by the vestibule on the side near the Labyrinth.

6 Enter the Labyrinth. After proceeding down as far as the figures of the fable of the Dog and the Ducks, turn back in order to leave on the side near Bacchus.

7 Go to see the Ballroom. Walk around it, go to the centre, and leave it to reach the bottom of the ascent and steps round Latona.

8 Go straight to the viewpoint below Latona; in passing, look at the small fountain of the Satyr in one of the bosquets. Once at this viewpoint, pause to consider the flights of steps, the vases, the statues, the lizards, Latona and the Château; and on the other side, the Royal Allée, Apollo, the Canal, the tall jets in the bosquets, Flora, Saturn, and Ceres on the right, Bacchus to the left.

9 Go down by the Girandole which you will see in passing on the way to Saturn. Walk half round Saturn, and go to the Royal Island.

10 Pass onto the causeway, where there are jets of water on both sides; walk round the large pool, and at the far end pause to consider the tall jets, the shells, the basins, the statues and the porticos.

KING LOUIS XIV (1638–1715)

*Manière de montrer les jardins de Versailles*

THE 20TH MAY the count gave a great fete at Bagatelle to the King and Queen and the court which was at this time at La Muette; here was the Superbe Band of Musick placed upon a scaffold on the thicket of trees which as the company walked round to see the Gardins played which with the echo of the trees made an enchanting affects and in differant parts of the wood was Booths made of the Branches of trees in which there was actors who acted differant pieces agreeable to the scene; on the further side towards Longchamp there was erected a Pyramide by which was a Marble tomb; this part of the wood being neuly taken in to the grounds there remained the wall of the bois de Boulogne and to render this scene More agreeable Mr. Belanger had an invention which made a Singulare effect by undermining the wall on the outside and placing people with ropes to pull the wall down at a word; at this pyramide there was an acteur who acted the part of a Majician who asked there Majestys how they liked the Gardins and what a beautifull vue there was towards the plaine if that wall did not obstruct it, but that there Majestys need only give the word that he with his inchanting wand would make that wall dissapear; the queen not knowing told him with a Laugh 'Very well I should wisht to see it disappear' and in the instant the signal was given and above 200 yards opposite where the company stood fell flat to the ground which surprised them all. This fete terminated with a ball in the Pavillion at which they all danced except the King who amuzed in playing

at Billiards at half a crown a game; at this rate he could never ruin his fortune; the whole terminated by illuminations all round the Gardin.

THOMAS BLAIKIE (1751–1838)

*Diary of a Scotch Gardener at the French Court*
*at the End of the Eighteenth Century*

# Vauxhall

. . .

ALTHOUGH THE GARDENS of Vauxhall have passed away as much as the gardens of Babylon, yet there is no need to describe what our young people saw on their visit to the first mentioned of these two places of splendid entertainment. Fond memory has not forgotten as yet all the delights and wonders of the Royal Gardens—

The hundred thousand extra lamps, which were always lighted; the fiddlers, in cocked-hats, who played ravishing melodies under the gilded cockleshell in the midst of the Gardens; the singers, both of comic and sentimental ballads, who charmed the ears there; the country dances, formed by bouncing cockneys and cockneyesses, and executed amidst jumping, thumping, and laughter; the signal which announced that Madame Saqui was about to mount skyward on a slack-rope ascending to the stars; the hermit that always sat in the illuminated hermitage; the dark walks, so favourable to the interviews of young lovers; the pots of stout handed about by the people in the shabby old liveries; and the twinkling boxes, in which the happy feasters made believe to eat slices of almost invisible ham.

WILLIAM MAKEPEACE THACKERAY (1811–63)

*Vanity Fair*

< Londoners from all walks of life enjoy the illuminated bandstand at Vauxhall.

## Forbidden Territory

· · ·

THE HEDGE ALLOWED us a glimpse, inside the park, of an alley bordered with jasmine, pansies, and verbenas, among which the stocks held open their fresh plump purses, of a pink as fragrant and as faded as old Spanish leather, while on the gravel-path a long watering-pipe, painted green, coiling across the ground, poured, where its holes were, over the flowers whose perfume those holes inhaled, a vertical and prismatic fan of infinitesimal, rainbow-coloured drops. Suddenly I stood still, unable to move, as happens when something appears that requires not only our eyes to take it in, but involves a deeper kind of perception and takes possession of the whole of our being. A little girl, with fair, reddish hair, who appeared to be returning from a walk, and held a trowel in her hand, was looking at us, raising towards us a face powdered with pinkish freckles. Her black eyes gleamed, and as I did not at that time know, and indeed have never since learned how to reduce to its objective elements any strong impression, since I had not, as they say, enough "power of observation" to isolate the sense of their colour, for a long time afterwards, whenever I thought of her, the memory of those bright eyes would at once present itself to me as a vivid azure, since her complexion was fair; so much so that, perhaps, if her eyes had not been quite so black—which was what struck one most forcibly on first meeting her—I should not have been, as I was, especially enamoured of their imagined blue.

I gazed at her, at first with that gaze which is not merely a messenger from the eyes, but in whose window all the senses assemble and lean out, petrified and anxious, that gaze which would fain reach, touch, capture, bear off in triumph the body at which it is aimed, and the soul with the body; then (so frightened was I lest at any moment my grandfather and father, catching sight of the girl, might tear me away from her, by making me run on in front of them) with another, an unconsciously appealing look, whose object was to force her to pay attention to me, to see, to know me. She cast a glance forwards and sideways, so as to take stock of my grandfather and father, and doubtless the impression she formed of them was that we were all absurd people, for she turned away with an indifferent and contemptuous air, withdrew herself so as to spare her face the indignity of remaining within their field of vision; and while they, continuing to walk on without noticing her, had overtaken and passed me, she allowed her eyes to wander, over the space that lay between us, in my direction, without any particular expression, without appearing to have seen me, but with an intensity, a half-hidden smile which I was unable to interpret, according to the instruction I had received in the ways of good breeding, save as a mark of infinite disgust; and her hand, at the same time, sketched in the air an indelicate gesture, for which, when it was addressed in public to a person whom one did not know, the little dictionary of manners which I carried in my mind supplied only one meaning, namely, a deliberate insult.

"Gilberte, come along; what are you doing?" called out in a piercing tone of authority a lady in white, whom I had not seen until that moment, while, a little way beyond her, a gentleman in a suit of linen "ducks," whom I did not know either, stared at me with eyes which seemed to be starting from his head; the little girl's smile abruptly faded, and, seizing her trowel, she made off without turning to look again in my direction, with an air of obedience, inscrutable and sly.

And so was wafted to my ears the name of Gilberte, bestowed on me like a talisman which might, perhaps, enable me some day to rediscover her whom its syllables had just endowed with a definite personality, whereas, a moment earlier, she had been only something vaguely seen. So it came to me, uttered across the heads of the stocks and jasmines, pungent and cool as the drops which fell from the green watering-pipe; impregnating and irradiating the zone of pure air through which it had passed, which it set apart and isolated from all other air, with the mystery of the life of her whom its syllables designated to the happy creatures that lived and walked and travelled in her company; unfolding through the arch of the pink hawthorn, which opened at the height of my shoulder, the quintessence of their familiarity—so exquisitely painful to myself—with her, and with all that unknown world of her existence, into which I should never penetrate.

MARCEL PROUST (1871–1922)

*Swann's Way*

# Improving Country Laborers

· · ·

SIR,

In your Gardener's Magazine, I have seen a paper on the benefits to be derived by the country labourer from a garden, and the means of teaching him how acquire those benefits, by William Stevenson, Esq.; and considering that it might of service to some of your readers, I shall endeavour to describe a method of teaching labourers to benefit by their gardens, which differs from Mr. Stevenson's, and which, in the hands of an indulgent master, I have in some measure been instrumental in effecting, when in the service of the late Lord Cawdor, of Stackpole Court, in Pembrokeshire.

His lordship, ever anxious to promote the comforts of his dependants, gave directions for additional chambers, and a better system of ventilation in his cottages; to repair the exterior in the cottage style, and build new ones where wanted. I was then instructed to put the gardens in a proper form behind each cottage, and to make a court in front, for the cultivation of flowers. I furnished them with such fruit-trees as were best adapted for that climate, and stocked their courts with herbaceous plants, shrubs, and creepers of the common kinds; informing the cottagers at the same time, that they would have to keep the whole in good order for the future; and I must here observe, that the information was not received with a good grace by some of them, prejudiced as they were against the introduction of any thing new.

Five premiums or rewards, of different value, were then offered to those who had the best cultivated garden, and most flowers in their courts, and about the 10th of August I inspected their gardens, and awarded the premiums. As the garden labourers, from the nature of their employment, had some advantage over the others, they were not allowed to compete with them, but were competitors among themselves; and the premiums were not confined to those who had had their gardens put in form for them but extended to the cottagers of the three parishes.

The successful candidates were so elated with the idea of having gained a prize, and the others flattered with the hope of doing the same the following season, that the spirit of gardening soon became general, and cuttings of fruit-trees, plants, and flower-seeds, were in great request with those very individuals who were most prejudiced against them at the formation of their little gardens.

The village of Stackpole was now frequented in the Summer season by the ladies and gentlemen of the neighbourhood, to see the flowers and improvements of the cottages; and many of the labourers, who had worked about the gardens for years, and never asked the name of a plant, began to ask the names of flowers that a certain lady or gentleman had admired the preceding day.

Two years before I left Stackpole Court, the premiums were discontinued, being considered unnecessary; and it was gratifying to see

that the cottagers paid the same attention to their gardens, in the evenings and mornings, as usual; they had experienced the comfort and advantage arising from so doing; for their fruit-trees were now in a bearing state, and their market for common fruits and early vegetables was tolerably good.

Having seen the desired effect accomplished, by the above method of teaching labourers to benefit by their gardens, I should be happy to hear of that, or a similar method, being adopted by those who have it in their power; and the poor man's cottage made comfortable and ornamental in scenery, instead of the leveling system which is practised by many.

I am, Sir, &c.

William Buchan, Blithfield, May 13th, 1826

WILLIAM BUCHAN

*Letter to Gardener's Magazine*

# A Garden in the Suburbs

. . .

WHAT PLEASURE HAVE not children in applying their little green watering-pans to plants in pots, or pouring water in at the roots of favourite flowers in borders? And what can be more rational than the satisfaction which the grown up amateur, or master of the house, enjoys, when he returns from the city to his garden in the summer evenings, and applies the syringe to his wall trees, with refreshing enjoyment to himself and the plants, and to the delight of his children, who may be watching his operations? What can be more refreshing than, in a warm summer's evening, to hear, while sitting in a cool par-lour, with the windows open, or in a summer-house, the showering of water by the syringe upon the leaves of the vines or fig trees trained under the adjoining veranda, or upon the orange trees and camellias, or other exotic shrubs, planted in the conservatory connects with it? What more delightful than to see the master or the mistress of a small garden or pleasure-ground, with all the boys and girls, the maids, and, in short, all the strength of the house, carrying pots and pails of water to different parts of the garden; and to see the refreshment produced to the soil and plants by the application of the watering-pan and syringe?

JOHN LOUDON (1783–1843)

*The Villa Gardener*

< Princess Victoria watering flowers at Kensington Palace

· · ·

ON LIGHT EVENINGS, after their tea-supper, the men worked for an hour or two in their gardens or on the allotments. They were first-class gardeners and it was their pride to have the earliest and best of the different kinds of vegetables. They were helped in this by good soil and plenty of manure from their pigsties; but good tilling also played its part. They considered keeping the soil constantly stirred about the roots of growing things the secret of success and used the Dutch hoe a good deal for this purpose. The process was called "tickling." "Tickle up old Mother Earth and make her bear!" they would shout to each other across the plots, or salute a busy neighbour in passing with "Just tickling her up a bit, Jack?"

The energy they brought to their gardening after a hard day's work in the fields was marvellous. They grudged no effort and seemed never to tire. Often, on moonlight nights in spring, the solitary fork of some one who had not been able to tear himself away would be heard and the scent of his twitch fire smoke would float in at the windows. It was pleasant, too, in summer twilight, perhaps in hot weather when water was scarce, to hear the *swish* of water on parched earth in a garden—water which had been fetched from the brook a quarter of a mile distant. "It's not good stintin' th' land," they would say. "If you wants anything out you've got to put summat in, if 'tis only elbow-grease."

The allotment plots were divided into two, and one half planted with potatoes and the other half with wheat or barley. The garden was

*a. Brassica capi=*
*Gestreiffter*
*b. Brassica capitata*
*tata purpurea et alba*
*Kopff=Kohl.*
*cum flore, Blühender Kopf=Kohl.*

reserved for green vegetables, currant and gooseberry bushes, and a few old-fashioned flowers. Proud as they were of their celery, peas and beans, cauliflowers and marrows, and fine as were the specimens they could show of these, their potatoes were their special care, for they had to grow enough to last the year round. They grew all the

old-fashioned varieties—ashleaf, kidney, early rose, American rose, magnum bonum, and the huge misshaped white elephant. Everybody knew the elephant was an unsatisfactory potato, that it was awkward to handle when paring, and that it boiled down to a white pulp in cooking; but it produced tubers of such astonishing size that none of the men could resist the temptation to plant it. Every year specimens were taken to the inn to be weighed on the only pair of scales in the hamlet, then handed round for guesses to be made of the weight. As the men said, when a patch of elephants was dug up and spread out, "You'd got summat to put in your eye and look at."

FLORA THOMPSON (1876–1947)

*Lark Rise*

# City Pride

. . .

TO JUDGE BY the present state of the garden, the last owner must have prided himself chiefly on his splendid show of canaries. Indeed, it would not surprise me to hear that he referred to his garden as "the back-yard." This would take the heart out of anything which was try-ing to flower there, and it is only natural that, with the exception of the three groundsel beds, the garden is now a wilderness. Perhaps "wilderness" gives you a misleading impression of space, the actual size of the pleasaunce being about two hollyhocks by one, but it is the correct word to describe the air of neglect which hangs over the place. However, I am going to alter all that.

With a garden of this size, though, one has to be careful. One cannot decide lightly upon a croquet-lawn here, an orchard there, and a rockery in the corner; one has to go all out for the one particular thing, whether it is the last hoop and the stick of a croquet-lawn, a mulberry-tree, or an herbaceous border...

At the back of my garden I have a high brick wall. To whom the bricks actually belong I cannot say, but at any rate I own the surface rights to this side of it. One of my ideas is to treat it as the back cloth of a stage, and paint a vista on it. A long avenue of immemorial elms, leading up to a gardener's lodge at the top of the wall—I mean at the end of the avenue—might create a pleasing impression. My work-room leads out into the garden, and I have a feeling that, if the door of this room were opened, and then hastily closed again on the plea that I mustn't be disturbed, a visitor might obtain such a glimpse of the avenue and the gardener's lodge as would convince him that I had come into property. He might even make an offer for the estate, if he were set upon a country house in the heart of London.

But you have probably guessed already the difficulty in the way of my vista. The back wall extends into the gardens of the householders on each side of me. They might refuse to co-operate with me; they might insist in retaining the blank ugliness of their walls, or endeavouring (as they endeavour now, I believe) to grow some unenterprising creeper up them; with the result that my vista would fail to create the necessary illusion when looked at from the side. This would mean that our guests would have to remain in one position, and that even in this position they would have to stand to attention—a state of things which might mar their enjoyment of our hospitality. Until, then, our neighbours give me a free hand with their segments of the wall, the vista must remain a beautiful dream.

However, there are other possibilities. Since there is no room in the garden for a watchdog *and* a garden, it might be a good idea to paint a phosphorescent and terrifying watchdog on the wall. Perhaps a watch-lion would be even more terrifying—and, presumably, just as easy to paint. Any burglar would be deterred if he came across a lion suddenly in the back garden. One way or another, it should be possible to have something a little more interesting than mere bricks at the end of the estate.

And if the worst comes to the worst—if it is found that no flowers (other than groundsel) will flourish in my garden, owing to lack of soil or lack of sun—then the flowers must be painted on the walls. This would have its advantages, for we should waste no time over the early and uninteresting stages of the plant, but depict it at once in its full glory. And we should keep our garden up to date. When delphiniums went out of season, we should rub them out and give you chrysanthemums; and if an untimely storm uprooted the chrysanthemums, in an hour or two we should have a wonderful show of dahlias to take their place. And we should still have the floor-space free for a sundial, or—if you insist on exercise—for the last hoop and the stick of a full-sized croquet lawn.

A.A. MILNE (1882  1956)
*If I May*

# Exile

###### . . .

WE HAVE BUMPED off the pavement onto a washboard road and there is a whirling storm of dust that flumes behind us. In the shaking of the truck and the buffeting of dust and wind, I can only breathe in short shallow gasps. The sides of the truck and the floor shake and bounce and the chains at the back clank in a Raggedy-Ann jig. I squeeze my eyes together against the wind and hold the corners of the truck, my arms outstretched. My dress flaps wildly. I am a flag fraying against the sky. Or a scarecrow or a skeleton in the wind.

"Where are we going?" I shout to Uncle.

He is sitting up straight like a sphinx on a box and staring at the land. We have come to the moon. We have come to the edge of the world, to a place of angry air. Was it just a breath ago that we felt the green watery fingers of the mountain air? Here, the air is a fist. I am leaning into the corner, a boxer cowering against the ropes. Uncle, his hands on his knees, is a statue beside me.

"Where are we going?" I shout again, moving along the edge of the truck, close to Uncle.

He nods but doesn't reply. The wind howls and guffaws at my eardrums.

Running along beside the wind-tunnel road is a ditch of brown water bordered with grass and weeds fluttering like laundry. On the miles of barbed-wire fences, there are found skull-shaped weeds slinging or occasionally careening off into the brown air. We keep heading straight down the road and we are the only thing moving on the earth.

When we stop finally, it is at the side of a small hut, like a tool shed, smaller even than the one we lived in in Slocan. We are at the far end of a large yard that has a white house in the middle. Between the shed and the farmer's house are some skeletons of farm machinery with awkward metal jaws angled upwards, like the remains of dinosaurs in a prehistoric battleground. There is a mound of earth beyond the machines which Uncle tells me later is a root cellar. The farmer's house is a real house with a driveway leading into a garage. It makes me think of our house in Vancouver though this is not as large. Through the whipping brown dust, I can see its white lace curtains in the window and its border of determined orange flowers. Our hut is at the edge of a field that stretches as far as I can see and is filled with an army of Spartan plants fighting in the wind. Every bit of plant growth here looks deliberate and fierce.

JOY KOGAWA (1935–)

*Obasan*

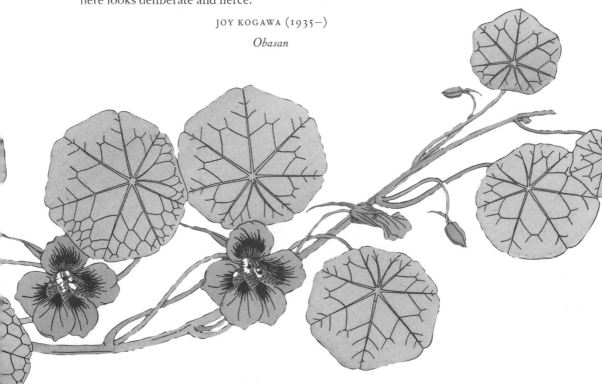

# *Neglect*

· · ·

THE SNOWFLAKES WERE just as heavy as the day before but dissolved where they landed on the wet ground. Paddy tightened her scarf around her head, keeping her hood up, and trudged up the steep hill to the Eastfield Star.

The Meehan family home was on a tiny council estate at the southeastern tip of Glasgow's sprawl. The estate had been built for a small community of forty or so miners working the now defunct Cambusland coal seam. From a central roundabout of houses, the five legs radiated out with six houses on each, some containing four flats, some freestanding with five bedrooms to accommodate large, extended families. Built in the cottage style, the houses had low-fronted gable ends, sloping roofs, and small windows.

The Meehans lived in Quarry Place, the first prong to the left on the Star. The two-story house was low and built so close to the soil that every room was slightly damp. Paddy's mother, Trisha, had to

bleach the skirting in the hall cupboard every three months to get the mold off it. Gray, eyeless silverfish had colonized the bathroom carpet, making a five-second pause necessary between flicking on the light and entering the room, giving them a head start in their slither off to dark places. Theirs wasn't a large house: Paddy shared a bedroom with Mary Ann, the boys got separate rooms after their sister Caroline's wedding, and their parents had a room.

Each of the Eastfield houses had a decent amount of land around it, a few feet of front garden and a hundred-foot strip at the back. Mr. Anderson on the roundabout grew onions and potatoes and rhubarb and other sour things that children wouldn't steal to eat, but the rest of the gardens were just scrub land, bald brown grass in the winter and thicker grass through the summer. Wooden fences hung to the side, and grass grew freely between the paving stones.

They were only two or three miles from the centre of Glasgow, close to wide-open fields and farms, but the families who lived on the Star were city people, workers in heavy industry, and didn't know how to tend gardens. Most found the persistent encroachment of nature bewildering and a little frightening. A tree had somehow grown at the bottom of the Meehans' garden. It had started growing before they arrived, and they'd mistaken it for a bush until it really took off. No one knew what kind of tree it was, but it got bigger and branchier every year.

DENISE MINA (1966–)

*Field of Blood*

# To Name Is to Possess

. . .

I DO NOT know the names of the plants in the place I am from (Antigua). I can identify the hibiscus, but I do not know the name of a white lily that blooms in July, opening at night, perfuming the air with a sweetness that is almost sickening, and closing up at dawn. There is a bush called whitehead bush; it was an important ingredient in the potions my mother and her friends made for their abortions, but I do not know its proper name; this same bush I often had to go and cut down and tie in bunches to make a broom for sweeping our yard; both the abortions and the sweeping of the yard, actions deep and shallow, in a place like that (Antigua) would fall into the category called Household Management. I had wanted to see the garden in Kingston so that I could learn the names of some flowers in the West Indies, but along with the salvia the garden had in it only roses and a single anemic-looking yellow lupine (and this surprised me, because lupine is a temperate zone flower and I had very recently seen it in bloom along the roadside of a town in Finland).

This ignorance of the botany of the place I am from (and am of) really only reflects the fact that when I lived there, I was of the conquered class and living in a conquered place; a principle of this condition is that nothing about you is of any interest unless the conqueror deems it so. For instance, there was a botanical garden not far from where I lived, and in it were plants from various parts of the then

---

< The wealthy appropriate the plants of others to create exotic
luxury in chilly climes, as in this Russian winter garden of 1851.

British Empire, places that had the same climate as my own: but as I remember, none of the plants were native to Antigua. The rubber tree from Malaysia (or somewhere) is memorable because in the year my father and I were sick at the same time (he with heart disease, I with hookworms), we would go and sit under this tree after we ate our lunch, and under this tree he would tell me about his parents, who had abandoned him and gone off to build the Panama Canal (though of course he disguised the brutality of this). The bamboo grove is memorable because it was there I used to meet people I was in love with. The botanical garden reinforced for me how powerful were the people who had conquered me; they could bring to me the botany of the world they owned.

JAMAICA KINCAID (1949–)

*My Garden (Book)*

# The Garden Party
. . .

AND AFTER ALL the weather was ideal. They could not have had a more perfect day for a garden-party if they had ordered it. Windless, warm, the sky without a cloud. Only the blue was veiled with a haze of light gold, as it is sometimes in early summer. The gardener had been up since dawn, mowing the lawns and sweeping them, until the grass and the dark flat rosettes where the daisy plants had been seemed to shine. As for the roses, you could not help feeling they understood that roses are the only flowers that impress people at garden-parties; the only flowers that everybody is certain of knowing. Hundreds, yes, literally hundreds, had come out in a single night; the green bushes bowed down as though they had been visited by archangels.

Breakfast was not yet over before the men came to put up the marquee.

"Where do you want the marquee put, mother?"

"My dear child, it's no use asking me. I'm determined to leave everything to you children this year. Forget I am your mother. Treat me as an honoured guest."

But Meg could not possibly go and supervise the men. She had washed her hair before breakfast, and she sat drinking her coffee in a green turban, with a dark wet curl stamped on each cheek. Jose, the butterfly, always came down in a silk petticoat and a kimono jacket.

"You'll have to go, Laura; you're the artistic one."

Away Laura flew, still holding her piece of bread-and-butter. It's so delicious to have an excuse for eating out of doors, and besides, she loved having to arrange things; she always felt she could do it so much better than anybody else.

Four men in their shirt-sleeves stood grouped together on the garden path. They carried staves covered with rolls of canvas, and they had big tool-bags slung on their backs. They looked impressive. Laura wished now that she was not holding that piece of bread-and-butter, but there was nowhere to put it, and she couldn't possibly throw it away. She blushed and tried to look severe and even a little bit short-sighted as she came up to them.

"Good morning," she said, copying her mother's voice. But that sounded so fearfully affected that she was ashamed, and stammered like a little girl, "Oh—er—have you come—is it about the marquee?"

"That's right, miss," said the tallest of the men, a lanky, freckled fellow, and he shifted his tool-bag, knocked back his straw hat and smiled down at her. "That's about it."

His smile was so easy, so friendly, that Laura recovered. What nice eyes he had, small, but such a dark blue! And now she looked at the others, they were smiling too. "Cheer up, we won't bite," their smile seemed to say. How very nice workmen were! And what a beautiful morning! She mustn't mention the morning; she must be business-like. The marquee.

"Well, what about the lily-lawn? Would that do?"

---

< An alcove for entertaining, as recommended in
John Buonarotti Papworth, *Hints on Ornamental Gardening*, 1832

And she pointed to the lily-lawn with the hand that didn't hold the bread-and-butter. They turned, they stared in the direction. A little fat chap thrust out his under-lip, and the tall fellow frowned.

"I don't fancy it," said he. "Not conspicuous enough. You see, with a thing like a marquee," and he turned to Laura in his easy way, "you want to put it somewhere where it'll give you a bang slap in the eye, if you follow me."

Laura's upbringing made her wonder for a moment whether it was quite respectful of a workman to talk to her of bangs slap in the eye. But she did quite follow him.

"A corner of the tennis-court," she suggested. "But the band's going to be in one corner."

"H'm, going to have a band, are you?" said another of the workmen. He was pale. He had a haggard look as his dark eyes scanned the tennis-court. What was he thinking?

"Only a very small band," said Laura gently. Perhaps he wouldn't mind so much if the band was quite small. But the tall fellow interrupted.

"Look here, miss, that's the place. Against those trees. Over there. That'll do fine."

Against the karakas. Then the karaka-trees would be hidden. And they were so lovely, with their broad, gleaming leaves, and their clusters of yellow fruit. They were like trees you imagined growing on a desert island, proud, solitary, lifting their leaves and fruits to the sun in a kind of silent splendour. Must they be hidden by a marquee?

They must. Already the men had shouldered their staves and were making for the place. Only the tall fellow was left. He bent down, pinched a sprig of lavender, put his thumb and forefinger to his nose and snuffed up the smell. When Laura saw that gesture she forgot all about the karakas in her wonder at him caring for things like that—caring for the smell of lavender. How many men that she knew would have done such a thing? Oh, how extraordinarily nice workmen were, she thought. Why couldn't she have workmen for her friends rather than the silly boys she danced with and who came to Sunday night supper? She would get on much better with men like these.

KATHERINE MANSFIELD (1888–1923)

*"The Garden-Party"*

## GARDENERS
## RAMPANT

*G*ARDENERS ARE as diverse as the gardens they create. Some gardeners study to perfect their skills. Others fall into gardening
accidentally and muddle along as best they can. There are those who
live to garden, and those who garden in spite of themselves. Some gardeners believe firmly in using whatever tools are to hand to bring the
natural world under control. Others observe the lessons Nature offers
about how best to make their gardens grow.

Those who garden in community allotments and pea patches swap
tips with their neighbors as they work. Growers of vegetables and

< An early-twentieth-century German card

perennials make the rounds of their neighborhoods, surreptitiously dropping off bags of zucchini or clumps of divided day lilies. Bouquets are gathered and proudly displayed at country fetes and church festivals. People pile into buses to tour the gardens of others, for fun, inspiration, and the satisfaction of knowing that garden woes visit even the most well tended of gardens.

Gardening can also be a solitary pursuit. Intent on their work, some gardeners shun neighborly chitchat to concentrate on never-ending garden improvements or on growing the perfect flower. Their focus may lead to odd experiments in garden-making or reveal personality traits that non-gardeners find unsettling. Many gardeners find that their gardens are, quite simply, where they feel most at home.

# *Obsession*

. . .

*Qi Biaojia exhausted his family fortune constructing*
*an elaborate garden in which to house his family's library.*

WHEN THE PROJECT began, all I desired were four or five structures.
But guests came by to pay their calls upon me there and, pointing
this way and that, they declared: "Here you should site a pavilion"
or "This site is perfect for a gazebo." I was unmoved by their com-
ments, objecting in my mind that this was not at all in keeping with
my own original intentions. After another turn or two through my
estate, however, unconsciously, I found myself most discomforted to
discover that their words had taken possession of my soul. Yes, indeed,
I could not be without that pavilion there or this gazebo here. And
before one stage of construction was completed, I found new ideas and
novel conceptions occurring to me at every turn. Whenever I came
to the end of a path or trod upon a dangerous track, I would tax my
mind to come up with unexpected conceits as if heavenly inspired, to
the extent that I would continue to do so even in my dreams. Thus,
as my enthusiasm for the project was roused, so too did my fascination for it grow more intense. I would set off there at the crack of
dawn to return only as the sun was setting. The various bothersome
family affairs that I was obliged to deal with I would now do so only
once the candles had been lit. Impatiently I would lie upon my pillow waiting for the dawn to shoot forth its first tongues of light where

upon I would order the serving lads to make ready my boat and set off, wishing all the time that the three *li* we had to cover to get to the site were but a single step away. I was heedless of the extreme cold or the scorching heat, the goose bumps on my flesh or the sweat that ran down my spine. Not even the most violent of storms could deter me from setting off in my boat each morning. When groping around at the head of my bed at night and finding that my cash reserve was exhausted, a sense of desolation would come over me. Yet the moment I reached the mountain again the next day and began to wander about I would worry that the rocks I had bought and the timber I had stored away were yet insufficient for the task at hand. Thus have I emptied my purse these past two years. I have fallen ill and then recovered; having recovered I have fallen ill again. This then is an account of my crazy obsession with the creation of my garden.

QI BIAOJIA (1602–45)

*"Footnotes to Allegory Mountain"*

# The Crop Dilemma

. . .

NEXT TO DECIDING where to start your garden, the most important matter is, what to put in it. It is difficult to decide what to order for dinner on a given day: how much more oppressive is it to order in a lump an endless vista of dinners, so to speak! For, unless your garden is a boundless prairie (and mine seems to me to be that when I hoe it on hot days), you must make a selection, from the great variety of vegetables, of those you will raise in it; and you feel rather bound to supply your own table from your own garden, and to eat only as you have sown.

I hold that no man has a right (whatever his sex, of course) to have a garden to his own selfish uses. He ought not to please himself, but every man to please his neighbour. I tried to have a garden that would give general moral satisfaction. It seemed to me that nobody could object to potatoes (a most useful vegetable); and I began to plant them freely. But there was a chorus of protest against them. "You don't want to take up your ground with potatoes," the neighbours said: "you can buy potatoes" (the very thing I wanted to avoid doing is buying things). "What you want is the perishable things that you cannot get fresh in the market."—"But what kind of perishable things?" A horticulturalist of eminence wanted me to sow lines of strawberries and raspberries right over where I had put my potatoes in drills. I had about five hundred strawberry-plants in another part of my garden; but this fruit-fanatic wanted me to turn my whole patch into vines and runners. I suppose I could raise strawberries enough for all my neighbours; and perhaps I ought to do it. I had a little space prepared for melons,—musk-melons,—which I showed to an experienced friend. "You are not going to waste your ground on musk-melons?" he asked. "They rarely ripen in this climate thoroughly, before frost." He had tried for years without luck. I resolved to not go into such a foolish experiment. But, the next day, another neighbour happened in. "Ah! I see you are going to have melons. My family would rather give up anything else in the garden than musk-melons,—of the nutmeg variety. They are the most grateful things we have on the table." So there it was. There was no compromise: it was melons or no melons, and somebody offended in any case. I half resolved to plant them a little late, so that they would, and they wouldn't. But I had the same difficulty about string-beans (which I detest), and squash (which I tolerate), and parsnips, and the whole round of green things.

I have pretty much come to the conclusion, that you have got to put your foot down in gardening. If I had actually taken counsel of my friends, I should not have had a thing growing in the garden to-day but weeds. And besides, while you are waiting, Nature does not wait. Her mind is made up. She knows just what she will raise, and she has an infinite variety of early and late. The most humiliating thing to me about a garden is the lesson it teaches of the inferiority of man. Nature is prompt, decided, inexhaustible. She thrusts up her plants with a vigour and freedom that I admire; and the more worthless the plant, the most rapid and splendid its growth. She is at it early and late, and all night; never tiring, nor showing the least sign of exhaustion.

E.A. BOWLES (1865–1954)

*My Garden in Summer*

A Swedish family plants vegetables at their summer home, 1919.

# Kleptomania in Ceylon

. . .

BY THE MID-THIRTIES both Lalla's and Rene's dairies had been wiped out by Rinderpest. Both were drinking heavily and both were broke.

We now enter the phase when Lalla is best remembered. Her children were married and out of the way. Most of her social life had been based at Palm Lodge but now she had to sell the house, and she burst loose on the country and her friends like an ancient monarch who had lost all her possessions. She was free to move wherever she wished, to do whatever she wanted. She took thorough advantage of everyone and had bases all over the country. Her schemes for organizing parties and bridge games exaggerated themselves. She was full of the "passions," whether drunk or not. She had always loved flowers but in her last decade couldn't be bothered to grow them. Still, whenever she arrived on a visit she would be carrying an armful of flowers and announce, "Darling, I've just been to church and I've stolen some

flowers for you. These are from Mrs. Abeysekare's, the lilies are from Mrs. Ratnayake's, the agapanthus is from Violet Meedeniya, and the rest are from *your* garden." She stole flowers compulsively, even in the owner's presence. As she spoke with someone her straying left hand would pull up a prize rose along with the roots, all so that she could appreciate it for that one moment, gaze into it with complete pleasure, swallow its qualities whole, and then hand the flower, discarding it, to the owner. She ravaged some of the best gardens in Colombo and Nuwara Eliya. For some years she was barred from the Hakgalle Public Gardens.

MICHAEL ONDAATJE (1943–)

*Running in the Family*

# A Most Awful Muddle

· · ·

THEY STEPPED DOWN flights of granite steps with two granite balls at the top and bottom of every meanest flight, into the dreadful complexity of Aunt Louisa's water-garden. This garden was designed with all the ingenuity of a formless mind. There was something almost invigorating in its awful failure to please. The whole thing was really the most stupendous failure. There was nothing about it that anyone could possibly commend. Even Aunt Louisa wondered about it a little at times, but she would still any query in her mind by buying another pot of bronze or stone or alabaster and disposing it in some fresh nook. Or she would buy another couple of Cyprus and pop them in somewhere. And there was always room for a new nymph, cherub, or bird-bath, and the establishment of these would reinstate both her interest and her confidence in her garden and herself. After all, grey stone and Nepita, water and pink water lilies—what could be more pretty and attractive? And it was marvellous how well palms did here in the mild winters. Yes, palms were here too, in all their want of propriety in any Irish garden. Everything that should not be was here. Balustradings in profusion entwined by pink rambler roses, impatiently waiting to burst into flower. Terra-cotta pots full of geraniums and lobelia flanking bronze Buddhas and stone bridges. No country was omitted in this rich horticultural mixture. Japan, Thibet, China, Venice, Greece, not a country or town that had not yielded its dash of inspiration to some mood of Aunt Louisa's vigorous mind.

In these days when so many people have such successions of good ideas about gardens and put them into execution with such practical efficiency, it comes as a kind of inverted pleasure to see a really good gross unbelievable muddle like this.

MOLLY KEANE (1904–96)

*Full House*

# *Retired*

. . .

THERE IS... A class of men, whose recreation is their garden. An individual of this class, resides some short distance from town—say in the Hampstead-road, or the Kilburn-road, or any other road where the houses are small and neat, and have little slips of back garden. He and his wife—who is as clean and compact a little body as himself—have occupied the same house ever since he retired from business twenty years ago. They have no family. They once had a son, who died at about five years old. The child's portrait hangs over the mantelpiece in the best sitting-room, and a little cart he used to draw about, is carefully preserved as a relic.

In fine weather the old gentleman is almost constantly in the garden; and when it is too wet to go into it, he will look out of the window at it, by the hour together. He has always something to do there, and you will see him digging, and sweeping, and cutting, and planting, with manifest delight. In spring-time, there is no end to the sowing of seeds, and sticking little bits of wood over them, with labels, which look like epitaphs to their memory; and in the evening, when the sun has gone down, the perseverance with which he lugs a great watering-pot about is perfectly astonishing. The only other recreation he has, is the newspaper, which he peruses every day, from beginning to end, generally reading the most interesting pieces of intelligence to his wife, during breakfast. The old lady is very fond of flowers, as the hyacinth-glasses in the parlour-window, and geranium-pots in the little front

< In a seed catalog, hope springs eternal.

court, testify. She takes great pride in the garden too: and when one of the four fruit-trees produces rather a larger gooseberry than usual, it is carefully preserved under a wine-glass on the sideboard, for the edification of visitors, who are duly informed that Mr. So-and-so planted the tree which produced it, with his own hands. On a summer's evening, when the large watering-pot has been filled and emptied some fourteen times, and the old couple have quite exhausted themselves by trotting about, you will see them sitting happily together in the little summerhouse, enjoying the calm and peace of the twilight, and watching the shadows as they fall upon the garden, and gradually growing thicker and more sombre, obscure the tints of their gayest flowers—no bad emblem of the years that have silently rolled over their heads, deadening in their course the brightest hues of early hopes and feelings which have long since faded away. These are their only recreations, and they require no more. They have within themselves, the materials of comfort and content; and the only anxiety of each, is to die before the other.

CHARLES DICKENS (1812–70)

*"London Recreations"*

# Conversations with the Gardener

. . .

GENERALLY, WHEN WE returned to the house, I had time before lun-cheon to escape for a quarter of an hour or so to the kitchen-garden, to have a chat with Williams. And at this particular moment I would find him in a very good mood, for he would just have finished his dinner. . . It was not that he talked much. . . but he. . . was versed in the ways of nature, human, animal, and floral, and could, as it were, feel the pulse of all green things. He possessed, too, a sort of rustic steadiness and calm, as do so many gardeners; for theirs is a profession which com-bines the best qualities both of those dedicated to the arts and of those engaged in manual labour. If it is difficult for a croupier or a pander to take an agreeable view of human endeavour, so, in the same way, it is not easy for a gardener to be anything but benevolent; his activi-ties never harm anyone, contain no trace of worldly—as apart from professional—ambition, and often he can obtain esthetic satisfaction from them as well. Moreover, Williams had an enchanting voice, with a burr to it, and, further, expecting my visit, he would nearly always have by him a marvel of some kind to show me, a freak blossom, some vegetable curiosity, a new plant in the hothouse, or some morels that a friend had found growing under a beech tree a few miles away; this last would most surely lead to an enjoyable discussion concerning edi-ble fungi (for, in the manner of all small boys, I loved best, next to asking questions, a discussion—so long as it was not of too abstract an order—concerning things about which I knew nothing). And at any

rate I was able to compare the morels with the blue-stalks that grow at Renishaw and were not found here; lovely fawn-coloured toadstools, shaped like a mandarin's umbrella, with amethystine interior linings, as full of colour as if their pleatings had been dyed in Tyrian purple—and an exact transposition into different terms of that other Derbyshire speciality, bluejohn. Sometimes he would grow almost angry as he extolled, in counter-attack, the merits of the brown and crumbly fungus of which he had constituted himself champion.

These arguments took place in the potting shed; the morels, done up in a red-and-yellow bandana, lay on a shelf near by. From nails on the wall great golden beards of bast rippled down to the floor, and the atmosphere seemed to contain in it the very secret of green growth, the very germ of life, a scent of sacking and bulbs and earth and warmth.

OSBERT SITWELL (1892–1969)

*The Scarlet Tree*

# *Peaches*

. . .

I GREW UP in southeastern Virginia, on the ocean. I had a boyhood full of intoxicating smells, of the soft spray from the ocean, the forceful perfume of gardenias, the scent of ripe figs wafting into the open window. In the summer, it was very hot, but often there was a wind from the ocean to make the heat bearable. Everything was more intense in the sun-drenched summer: roses, the crisp grass dehydrated by the heat, fat bees languidly treading air, even the mockingbirds. Before I was old enough to go to school, I walked around barefoot from May to October. I knew every plant and bush and flower, everything that grew near our house, from all sides. There were no barriers between me and the earth. I *was* the summer.

21

The first gardener I ever met was a black man. His name was Ford, and he worked for my grandmother. When she came from her house in Norfolk to stay with us during the summer, Ford came, too. I was never happier than to see him arrive every May. He was a quiet, hardworking man with lovely, peat-colored skin who spent long hours in the fierce summer sun working on the plants and shrubs and flowers in our yard. He was both a father and a mother figure to me, tolerant and accepting. I used to follow him around for hours in the hot Virginia day. Remembering how hard he worked and how thoroughly—I can

*Alberge jaune.*

still see the sweat dripping down his neck and cheeks, the small veins bulging on his forehead, a bandanna curled around his neck—I'm sure I was a distraction, if not a downright nuisance. But he never excluded me. He made me feel a part of his task.

What fascinated me about Ford even as a little boy was the boldness with which he worked. He snipped and cut our peach tree so deftly and rapidly it frightened me. "Won't that kill the tree if you do that, Ford?" I asked him as he pruned the tree. "No, boy. This is going to *help* this peach tree." Branches and twigs flew off the tree with a blinding rapidity as his scissors darted here and there and everywhere. There might have been a logic somewhere, but I couldn't find it. "But, Ford, how do you know *what* to cut?" I pleaded. He bent down and cut off a huge branch. He'd cut too much! I squealed and looked down in horror at the large crooked arm, leaves still on it. Ford stood back up. "I just know, boy."

And, indeed, later that summer we had big fat pink peaches, globes hanging everywhere from that tree. And they exploded with deliciousness.

RICHARD GOODMAN (1945–)
*French Dirt*

< Peaches travelled from China to the New World.

# The Lethal Garden

. . .

THE LONDON GARDEN, dank, dark and filled with foul humours is, of course, under the influence of Saturn; ergo, plants of saturnine humour flourish therein. Most plants which seek obscurity and putrefaction for their habitat are poisonous in some degree, some so eminently so that they may do actual harm to pets (oh joy!) or children (alleluia!).

Plant-men tend to guard this secret jealously, preferring to stress the benignity of "Dame Flora," rather than to advertise to all and sundry that by buying their aconitum the gardener is actually providing himself with the source of one of the most deadly narcotic alkaloids known to man. A casual touch of the leaves will irritate the skin and the pollen inflames the eyes. Planted where the neighbours' children jump down into your garden, it will exact revenge a dozen-fold.

*Aconitum napellus,* monkshood, is rather beautiful, although the blue flowers have the expression of a sort of frozen scream. Its steeples combine well with the flat, bat-shaped leaves of *Atropa belladonna,* deadly nightshade (called in this household by obscure family tradition deadly nightshirt), whose brilliantly black berries are very attractive (and fatal) to children. This bedding scheme needs only the fine-cut and wonderfully poisonous leaves of *Conium maculatum,* hemlock, and the downy leaves and purple-veined flowers of henbane, *Hyoscyamus niger,* to turn your dreary lightwell or back area into a fascinating chamber of horrors.

The lethal garden can be given further interest by tasteful plantings of hellebore, *foetidus, viridis* and *niger,* all readily available, violently purgative and utterly poisonous. I have a soft spot too for *Caltha palustris,* the marsh marigold, who adores life in W.10 and is quite poisonous, and *Anemone nemorosa* (poisonous, acid and blistering) and the other charming members of the *ranunculaceae* who are venomous, especially the celery-leaved buttercup, *Ranunculus sceleratus.*

The crown of the murderer's garden is that most hypnotically horrible of vegetable phenomena, *Colchicum autumnale,* the autumn flowering crocus. Its luminous naked flower, the colour of anaemic gums, appears without leaves as the autumn light is fading and everything else is dying back. In its corms this vile thing harbours colchicine, an alkaloid which does not simply kill. The utterly diabolical gardener can try soaking his flower seeds in it to produce monstrous chromosomal mutations.

GERMAINE GREER WRITING AS ROSE BLIGHT (1939–)

*The Revolting Garden*

There's a plant for every garden, no matter how inhospitable the landscape.

# Desert Design

. . .

A TERMITE IS one of those remarkably social insects whose ability to cooperate with one another is typically viewed with either admiration or fear, depending on whether one is an academic entomologist or a homeowner. Despite the fact that I belong to both camps, my predominant emotion falls heavily on the admiration side of the equation, especially because I believe that the little termites in the front yard belong to the native species *Gnathamitermes perplexus,* which is said to favor dead grasses, dried twigs and stems, and fallen cholla cactus bits, in which case they will probably leave the lumber in our house alone. Or so I hope.

Confident enough of our termites' harmless nature, I have encouraged them to stay around by serving up a number of large, dried cowpats, the crème de la crème of termite chow, as far as *Gnathamitermes* are concerned. Fortunately for them, if not for the rest of us, cow dung is a feature of almost every corner of the Sonoran Desert of Arizona (and Mexico), due to the affection that Arizonan (and Mexican) ranchers have for cows, huge numbers of which feed on private and public lands throughout the West.

In fact, my initial motivation for dropping cowpies onto the front yard had nothing to do with charity toward termites. Instead, I wanted a front yard with a true desert feel, and since cattle and their byproducts are universal in the Sonoran Desert, I knew I had to import a few cowpies to attach the seal of authenticity to my creations. When I go out walking in the Superstitions or Mazatzals, I keep my eye open for just the right cowpats to bring home. A highly rated one must be dry and odorless but not so old as to be falling apart. It must be attractively circular rather than asymmetric, and big, at least a foot in diameter and preferably closer to eighteen inches. Given the dominance of cows in the desert, I rarely have to hunt far for these treasures, which go into my daypack for later positioning by a paloverde or fairy duster in my yard.

My wife tells me that several neighbors have taken her aside to speak of the cowpies in our front yard. They claim to be unconcerned about their effect on local real estate values but rather wonder if I had a completely normal childhood.

JOHN ALCOCK (1942–)

*In a Desert Garden*

39

MEETING THE SENATOR like that and knowing that he was probably on his way to judge the Flower Show made Mr. Oliver feel just a little sick. He had been wonderfully relieved when they had all hurried on their way. It would not have looked good for him to be seen talking with the Senator just before the judging. Not at all.

And he must *not* go near the Grain Exhibits and Handicrafts Building where the flowers would be judged, either. In many ways showing flowers was difficult. It had been a long day since he had got up and walked over his lawn to the flower beds and Walter's cross. He must make a careful selection before the sun had come up to fade their colour, wilt a petal, or carry a prize flower past the peak of its bloom. He had cut his gladioli two days before, just as a tip of colour was peeking through the green bud sheath; he had hung them down in the cool darkness of the basement; he was not worried about how his gladioli would do. They were sure.

Roses. It had been a good snapdragon year; he had six sprays of that lovely bronze variety—straight, close, fat crowing blossoms, the colour like shot silk. He picked six lavender sweet peas for the "Six—One Colour" section, and for the "Six—Mixed" he had half a dozen long-stemmed ones, each with five blossoms. No. Snapdragons and gladioli and sweet peas did not worry him. Roses. They did.

He looked out past Walter's cross and to the brilliant part beyond where the gladioli lifted, each with a lath stake to hold it from the distorting influence of the wind, dogs, small children, and the inexplicable, uncooperative will of nature, which insisted on directing them in every way but the right one: straight up. The stakes were marked in careful printing: Maiden Mist, Sir Wilfrid Laurier, Florence Nightingale, Queen Elizabeth. Then there was a gloriously salmon flower tinting in its ruffled edges to pink; it had been a sport three years ago from a common pink variety, and he had nursed it through the bulblet stage to this climactic year. Upon *its* lath stake was printed *Minnie*. It was Minnie Oliver's favourite.

Roses had become more and more satisfying. They challenged in this country. Actually gladioli were the easiest to get results with, if one trenched and irrigated, keeping the chill town water off the plants themselves. But for all their flashy brilliance, they were not his favourite. Roses were.

He looked down now at the rosary part of the garden, where among the coarser bush roses bloomed the Brahmin of all the plants he'd grown, the first hybrid tea he had ever been able to bring through a winter. He had trenched it, mulched it, soaked and frozen it for the winter; he had sprayed it, fed and fertilized it; he had pruned it, staked it, dusted it, and now it had produced among the others one superlative bloom which, cut at this precise moment, would be excellently right by late this afternoon, when the judging would take place. He bent over it, saw that it held still a clear bead of dew that trembled as he clipped the stem. It was a pity the drop would not be cradled there when the judges looked at it in the Grain Exhibits and Handicrafts Building...

In the afternoon's excitement there had not been time for the news to travel far, so that to most of the audience Harry's announcement came as a complete surprise.

"Winner of the Grand Championship ribbon of the twenty-third Annual Perennial and Annual Flower Show—Mrs. Mame Napolean."

Mame, seated with Rory and the children in the front of the grandstand, was startled. When she had left Penny Novelty with the rosebush to take the kids to the picture show, she had left the thing behind and had to go back into the theatre. She would have forgotten it again on the bus seat if Byron hadn't picked it up and carried it home with him. There she dropped it by the door on the south side of the house, intending to stick it into the ground somewhere or other the next morning. For over a week it had lain forgotten on the goat manure piled against that side of the house for winter insulation. Had it not been so strategically placed that it caught the thrown contents of the slop bucket and the washbasin whenever she went to the back door, or if it had not been by Elvira's play spot where she spent engrossed mornings and afternoons digging with an old tablespoon to fill and empty and fill again the rusty pot her mother had given her, it might have perished for want of moisture—or from the hunger of the goats that steered clear of Elvira, always.

Even the young shoots that had sprouted in the sun had weathered the nights of frost, for compassionate warmth breathed up from the rotting goat manure on which it lay. Then one morning on her way to the woodpile she noticed it; at the same time she saw the tablespoon

*Fig 1.* ROSA *rubra plena, spinosissima, pedunculo musoso Boerh. Ind. alt. 2. 252.*
*Fig 2.* ROSA *prænestina, variegata plena Hort. Eÿ.*

excavation Elvira had made the afternoon before. The thing might as well go in there. She tore the burlap from its roots and held the plant upright in the hole while she filled in and patted dirt and goat manure around it.

With its southern exposure, and the careless daily baths of wash and slop water filtering down almost hundred-proof goat manure to the roots, the plant rallied. It had already served the normal tea-rose span of life in a city greenhouse, forced under glass and tropical steam heat to contribute long- and slender-stemmed blooms to tea parties and corsages, hospital rooms and wedding bouquets, boutonnieres and funeral wreaths. Considered almost spent, it had been uprooted and wrapped with others to be shipped out and sold cheaply for whatever dregs of energy remained in it.

Through June it had produced dark and leathery green leaves. For a while Mame and the children had watched for the appearance of buds, but they had soon tired of this, and left the rose to sun, slop

water, goat manure, and its own devices. She could quite honestly say she hadn't given the goddam thing another thought till this very morning. When they had all left for the fair, she had glanced back and seen the one rose from the gate, had told Rory to wait while she ran into the house and got the tomato soup tin. In spite of the goats, and Elvira, it had produced one yellow rose. She might as well enter it in the flower show.

Now, as she took the cup from Harry, Byron standing beside her, his pant laces dangling, the blue ribbon flowing down his shirt where he'd pinned it as soon as his mother had handed it to him, she looked out into the pale pond of upturned faces in the dusk before her. She supposed a person ought to say something; everybody did when they won something. She pulled her beret down more over her ears.

"It wasn't us," she said in her hoarse, carrying voice. "Just luck, I guess. I got it at the Penny Novelty when I took the kids to the clinic last spring. So I guess it was just luck—an'—an' goat manoor."

W.O. MITCHELL (1914–98)
*Roses Are Difficult Here*

# The Herbaceous Border

. . .

THE LONG HERBACEOUS border grew more and more interesting. A broad-leafed plant had been sending up tall stems, now it opened out and a big daisy-like blossom of yellow shone in the sun. "Leopard's bane," said old Griggs with decision, and "doronicum," said the Master, both being right, but I know not why it was considered a bane or healing, for the banes among the flowers are surely blessings. But here it was, and very grateful and comforting at this early time of year. As though conscious that a friendly eye had begun to watch over them, the scattered old plants of polyanthus, wall-flower, a group or so of tulips and some clumps of London pride brushed up this spring and cheered the eye.

I was studying the shooting green clumps, lilies here and there, golden rod, autumn daisy, maybe a stray phlox, many, very much too many, evening primroses, seedlings of self-sown foxgloves, and wondering how to rearrange them and make room for the better company I intended introducing, when his Reverence's Young Man came down the path laden with a big brown hamper. He looked quite excited.

"Oh, Mistress Mary, do come and examine the contents. I hope you may find welcome strangers here. I told my mother you needed anything and everything except geraniums. Was that right? So she has sent this hamper with instructions to get them in at once."

The Young Man was cutting away at string and fastenings, and rapidly strewing the path with big clumps of roots in which a careful hand had stuck a label.

I was divided between joy and reproof.

"How kind of her! But you should not have bothered her. How nice to have such, big, ready-grown plants! But why did you do it?"

"Mayn't I help the garden to grow? My mother promises more in the autumn; it appears flowers like to move just before winter."

"It is kind of you. This border is such a weight on my mind. It needs so much, I think. And what a lot the hamper holds!"

"Let me do the dirty work," cried the Young Man, as I hauled out a big root. "You shall tell me where to plant them."

"The earth isn't dirty, it is beautifully, healthily clean; and don't you love its 'most excellent cordial smell'? Shall I get Griggs and a spade?"

"Oh, why bother Griggs? Won't I do as well? I know nearly as much and am twice as willing."

"Yes, but think of—"

"Don't say parish. There is only old Mrs. Gunnet and she will keep. These plants demand immediate attention. My mother was most emphatic about that."

It is very difficult to have a conscience as well as a garden and to keep both in good working order. I could not think Mrs. Gunnet and her rheumatism as important as my garden; moreover, I felt I was carrying out the teaching of Tolstoy in bringing man and his Mother Earth into direct contact.

"Griggs could not come anyhow, he is digging a grave," I said con-
clusively. "Let us do it."

So the Young Man fetched a selection of gardening implements
and we both set to work, he to dig and I to instruct.

"This is delphinium," I cried joyfully, handing him a big clump,
"dark blue, I want it badly." And in answer to an inquiring look, for
the Young Man knew less, much less, than I did, "That is larkspur and
it is a perennial, and this jolly big root means plenty of spikes."

"Spikes!" he echoed, patting the roots vigorously.

"Those tall spikes of flowers, you know, very blue. One looks so
lonely all by itself."

"Ah! That is a way we all have, we poor solitary ones."

"These are penstemons. They are, well, I forget, but I know I want them. Suppose we put them further forward; they don't look like growing so tall. Gaillardias, ah! I know, they are brilliant and effective. I bought some seeds to suit the others. These will save time. Now, a big hole; this is Tritoma. What on earth is that? I have heard Grandis means big but Tritoma?"

We both studied the label.

"Must it have another name? Is that the rule? I told my mother the gardener was an Ignoramus. She might have written in the vulgar tongue."

"Did you mean me or Griggs?"

"Griggs, of course."

"Then you were wrong. But I remember now, I was studying its picture this morning in the catalogue. Tritoma stands for red-hot poker. It will look fine at the back."

"Well, you are getting on," said the Young Man, in tones of admiration. "But why won't they say 'poker' and have done with it?"

"I wish they would. It is very trying of them. See what a lot you are learning. This is much more improving for a son of Adam than visiting old women and babies."

"*Much!* And I like it much better, which shows it is good for me."

MAUD MARYON, 1900

*How the Garden Grew*

## PURELY
## FOR PLEASURE

"THE BEST purpose of a garden," wrote Gertrude Jekyll in 1901, "is to give delight." And delight is something that gardens give in abundance. Gardens engage not only sight but hearing, touch, smell, and taste. They are places where life can be lived: secret spaces explored, romances started, books read, friends entertained.

Those with patience and an artistic turn of mind can absorb themselves in the task of beautifying their gardens. The Chinese and the Japanese developed the art of miniaturizing trees, creating tiny landscapes of exquisite artistry. Bonsai is an art for experts, but even the

< Sir Francis Bacon (1561–1626) extolled the garden
as "the purest of human pleasures."

amateur can find amusement in garden embellishment. In 1754, in County Wexford, Ireland, Catherine Poer, Countess of Tyrone, recorded that she had spent 261 days decorating the interior of her grotto with shells.

Gardens allow the imagination to run riot on a grand scale, as well. In the mid-sixteenth century, Vicino Orsini created a horror garden at Bomarzo, Italy; a giant opens his mouth wide to eat the guests who dare enter the cave he protects. On a lighter note, the *giochi d'acqua,* or water tricks, of Italian Renaissance gardens splashed unsuspecting visitors. In France, around the same time, guests were entertained with music at Saint-Germain-en-Laye, as water in the Organ Grotto powered a smiling nymph whose fingers hit the keyboard while Mercury played the trumpet and a cuckoo came out to listen.

Gardens can be the perfect place to throw a party. The Mughal emperor Jahangir, who ruled from 1605 to 1627, gave a wine entertainment in his Shah-ara garden in Kabul for his close friends. When enough wine had been drunk, the emperor challenged his guests to jump over the stream that ran through the garden. Most of them fell in, although Jahangir—still spry at forty—made it safely across. At a party for Pope Gregory XIII at the Villa Lante in 1578, fireworks conjured up a dragon breathing flames. In 1640, Zheng Yuanxun, Secretary in the Bureau of Operations of the Ministry of War of the Ming Dynasty in China, hosted a party to celebrate the flowering of a single unusual yellow tree peony. The guests ate, drank, and composed poems; the winner of the poetry contest was awarded a golden goblet.

Even without grand celebrations, people enjoy touring gardens. Over the centuries, around the world, private estates have often been open for public viewing. During the late eighteenth and early nineteenth centuries, Hawkstone Park in Shropshire received more than ten thousand visitors a year. Its dramatic red sandstone cliffs were laid out with pathways that led past rock formations similar to those at the Syrian city of Palmyra, past the wax effigy of a neighbor's ancestor in a grotto, and on to a hermitage complete with a live "hermit." Not all gardens are so startling; some offer quiet spaces for restful enjoyment. Today, elderly gentlemen in blue and brown cotton jackets gather in the tranquil, cobbled courtyards of the Qu Shui, or Zigzagging Channel, garden in a modern suburb of Shanghai to play mah-jongg and sip from their thermoses of tea. This former temple garden, built in 1745, is dwarfed now by the soaring concrete skyscrapers of the fast-growing city.

Gardens can be visited over and over again, because every garden changes subtly each time a visitor returns. A gentle rain enhances the aroma of pine and roses; sunlight creates textures of shade; a carpet of snow scrunches underfoot; frost rimes leaves with a tracery of ice that dissolves to the touch; freshly plucked berries stain the tongue. Winter is quiet; spring full of promise. Summer hums, and fall ushers in sharp colors and crisp sounds. A tiny sapling grows into a stately tree that will eventually topple or, perhaps, be removed to create room for more garden experiments. The Jacobean writer William Lawson enticed his readers to consider all the delightful elements a garden can contain— flowers, fruit, wooded walks, topiary, mazes, places to exercise, and fragrant herbs. And not to forget a seat for relaxing and a brood of nightingales to fill the air with song.

No matter how grand or simple, no matter where it is found in the world, the garden is somewhere people come to celebrate the joys of life and find shelter from their cares. Pope or warrior, countess or pensioner, suburbanite, transient, or farmer, we all have gardens of which we dream.

# Planning a Pleasure Garden

. . .

THE SIGHT IS in no way so pleasantly refreshed as by fine and close grass kept short. It is impossible to produce this except with rich and firm soil; so it behoves the man who would prepare the site for a pleasure garden, first to clear it well from the roots of weeds, which can scarcely be done unless the roots are first dug out and the site leveled, and the whole well flooded with boiling water so that the fragments of roots and seeds remaining in the earth may not by any means sprout forth. Then the whole plot is to be covered with rich turf of flourishing grass, the turves beaten down with broad wooden mallets and the plants of grass trodden into the ground until they cannot be seen or scarcely anything of them perceived. For then little by little they may spring forth closely and cover the surface like a green cloth.

Care must be taken that the lawn is of such a size that about it in a square may be planted every sweet-smelling herb such as rue, and sage and basil, and likewise all sorts of flowers, as the violet, columbine, lily, rose, iris and the like. So that between these herbs and the turf, at the edge of the lawn set square, let there be a higher bench of turf flowering and lovely; and somewhere in the middle provide seats so that men may sit down there to take their repose pleasurably when their senses need refreshment. Upon the lawn too, against the heat of the sun, trees should be planted or vines trained, so that the lawn may have a delightful and cooling shade, sheltered by their leaves. For from these trees shade is more sought after than fruit, so that not much trouble should be taken to dig about and manure them, for this might cause great damage to the turf. Care should also be taken that the trees are not too close together or too numerous, for cutting off the breeze may do harm to health. The pleasure garden needs to have a free current of air along with shade. It also needs to be considered that the trees should not be bitter ones whose shade gives rise to diseases, such as the walnut and some others; but let them be sweet trees, with perfumed flowers and agreeable shade, like grapevines, pears, apples, pomegranates, sweet bay trees, cypresses and such like.

Behind the lawn there may be great diversity of medicinal and scented herbs, not only to delight the sense of smell by their perfume but to refresh the sight with the variety of their flowers, and to cause admiration at their many forms in those who look at them. Let rue be set in many places among them, for the beauty of its green foliage and also that its biting quality may drive away noxious vermin from the garden. There should not be any trees in the middle of the lawn, but rather let its surface delight in the open air, for the air itself is then more health-giving. If the [midst of the lawn] were to have trees planted on it, spiders' webs stretched from branch to branch would interrupt and entangle the faces of the passers-by.

If possible a clear fountain of water in a stone basin should be in the midst, for its purity gives much pleasure. Let the garden stand open to the North and East, since those winds bring health and cleanliness; to the opposite winds of the South and West it should be closed, on account of their turbulence bringing dirt and disease: for although the North wind may delay the fruit, yet it maintains the spirit and protects health. It is then delight rather than fruit that is looked for in the pleasure garden.

ALBERTUS MAGNUS (CA. 1200—80)

*On Vegetables and Plants*

## An Abbey Garden

. . .

I HAVE A garden filled with scented flowers in which flourish roses, violets, thyme, crocus, lilies, narcissi and rosemary. Other flowers appear in their season so that at Bourgueil spring is perpetual. No sooner does one flower fade than another takes its place. I have a sweet-flowing stream to water my garden. Transparent waves splash over marble pebbles and lose themselves after thousands of detours in the middle of a meadow. When the sun's rays beat down I can shelter my weary guests in agreeable shade. Bourgueil has a grove in which grow willows, sweet bay and myrtle, where the pear intermingles with olives, cherries or apples.

BAUDRY, ABBOT OF BOURGUEIL (1046–1130)

> Saint Fiacre is the patron saint of gardeners.

## A Warrior's Retreat

. . .

IN 914 [1508–09], I had constructed a charbagh garden called Bagh-i-Wafa on a rise to the south of the Adinapur fortress. It overlooks the river, which flows between the fortress and the garden. It yields many oranges, citrons, and pomegranates. [In 1524], the year I defeated Pahar Khan and conquered Lahore and Dipalpur, I had a banana tree brought and planted. It thrived. The year before that, sugarcane had been planted, some of which was being sent to Badakhshan and Bukhara. The ground is high, with constant running water, and the weather is mild in winter. In the middle of the garden is a small hill from which a one-mill stream always flows through the garden. The *charchaman* in the middle of the garden is situated atop the hill. In the southwest portion of the garden is a ten-by-ten pool surrounded by orange trees and some pomegranate trees. All around the pool is a clover meadow. The best place in the garden is there. . .

We moved out on Thursday the eighteenth and stopped in Bahar and Panjgram, reaching Bagh-i-Wafa the next morning. It was a time of beauty in the Bagh-i-Wafa. The open spaces were full of clover, and the pomegranate trees had turned a beautiful autumnal bright yellow. The fruit on the trees was bright red, and the orange trees were green and fresh, filled with innumerable oranges, although they were less yellow than one might wish. The pomegranates were quite good, but not so good as the best ones of our country. . . The three or four days we were in the garden the soldiers ate pomegranates to excess.

On Monday we left the garden. I stayed until the first watch and had some oranges gathered. Shah-Hasan was given the oranges of two trees. Some begs were given the oranges of one tree each, and others were given a half-share. Since I planned to tour Laghman that winter, I ordered about twenty orange trees around the pool kept in reserve...

On Saturday we got on a raft, went through the Darunta narrows, and disembarked above Jahannumay... We stopped in the Bagh-i-Wafa. The oranges had turned a beautiful yellow, and the greenery was full... We stayed in the Bagh-i-Wafa for five or six days. Having vowed to give up drinking at age forty, with only one year left to my fortieth year I was drinking to excess out of anxiety.

On Sunday the sixteenth [January 7, 1520], I had a morning draught, got sober, and had some ma'jum. Mulla Yarak played a tune he had composed in the *panjgah* mode on a *mukhammas*. He had composed quite nicely. I had not indulged in such diversions for a long time, and I too was tempted to create something. Shortly thereafter I wrote an air in the chargah mode...

On Wednesday, after my morning draught, I said in jest that anyone who sang a song in Persian would be allowed to drink a cup of wine. Lots of people drank on that account. Early that morning we sat under some willow trees in the middle of the meadow. Then it was proposed that anyone who sang a song in Turkish would be allowed to drink a cup. Many also drank on that account. When the sun was well up, we went to the edge of the pool under the orange trees and drank.

BABUR (1483–1530)

*The Baburnama: Memoirs of Babur, Prince and Emperor*

# Rekindling Love

### · · ·

THERE WAS A heavy fall of snow. In the evening there were new flurries. The contrast between the snow on the bamboo and the snow on the pines was very beautiful. Genji's good looks seemed to shine more brightly in the evening light.

"People make a great deal of the flowers of spring and the leaves of autumn, but for me a night like this, with a clear moon shining on snow, is the best—and there is not a trace of color in it. I cannot describe the effect it has on me, weird and unearthly somehow. I do not understand people who find a winter evening forbidding." He had the blinds raised. The moon turned the deepest recesses of the garden a gleaming white. The flower beds were wasted, the brook seemed to send up a strangled cry, and the lake was frozen and somehow terrible. Into this austere scene he sent little maidservants, telling them that they must make snowmen. Their dress was bright and their hair shone in the moonlight. The older ones were especially pretty, their jackets and trousers and ribbons trailing off in many colors, and the fresh sheen of their hair black against the snow. The smaller ones quite lost themselves in the sport. They let their fans fall most immodestly from their faces. It was all very charming. Rather outdoing themselves, several of them found that they had a snowball which they could not budge. Some of their fellows jeered at them from the east veranda. . .

The moon was yet brighter, the scene utterly quiet.

"The water is stilled among the frozen rocks.

A clear moon moves into the western sky."

Bending forward to look out at the garden, she was incomparably lovely. Her hair and profile called up most wonderfully the image of Fujitsubo, and his love was once again whole and undivided.

MURASAKI SHIKIBU (CA. 973–CA. 1014)

*Tale of Genji*

WHAT CAN YOUR eye desire to see, your ears to hear, your mouth to take, or your nose to smell, that is not to be had in an Orchard, with abundance of variety? What more delightsome than an infinite variety of sweet smelling flowers, decking with sundry colours, the green mantle of the earth, the universal mother of us all, so by them bespotted, so died, that all the World cannot sample them, and wherein it is more fit to admire the Dyer, than imitate his Workmanship, colouring not only the earth, but decking the air, and sweetning every breath and spirit.

The Rose red, Damask, Velvet, and double double Province-Rose, the sweet Musk-Rose double and single, the double and single white-

Rose: The fair and sweet-senting Woodbine, double and single, and double double. Purple Cowslips, and double Cowslips, and double double Cowslips, Primrose double and single. The Violet nothing behind the best, for smelling sweetly. A thousand more will provoke your content.

And all these by the skill of your Gardiner, so comelily and orderly 257 placed in your borders and squares, and so intermingled, that one looking thereon, cannot but wonder to see, what Nature, corrected by Art, can do.

When you behold in divers corners of your Orchard *Mounts* of stone or wood, curiously wrought within and without, or of earth covered with Fruit-trees, Kentish Cherries, Damsons, Plums, *&c.* with stairs of precious workmanship; and in some corner (or more) a true Dial or Clock, and some Antick works; and especially silver-sounding Musick, mixt Instruments, and Voices, gracing all the rest: How will you be wrapt with Delight?

Large Walks, broad and long, close and open, like the *Tempe*-groves in *Thessaly*, raised with gravel and sand, having seats and banks of Camomile; all this delights the mind, and brings health to the body.

View now with delight the works of your own hands, your Fruit-trees of all sorts, loaden with sweet blossoms, and fruit of all tastes, operations, and colours: your trees standing in comely order, which way soever you look.

Your borders on every side hanging and dropping with Feberries, Raspberries, Barberries, Currans, and the Roots of your trees pow-

dered with Strawberries, Red, White and Green, what a pleasure is this! Your Gardner can frame your lesser wood to the shape of men armed in the field, ready to give battle; of swift-running Grey-hounds, or of well-sented and true-running Hounds to chase the Deer, or hunt the Hare. This kind of hunting shall not waste your Corn, nor much your Coyn.

Mazes well framed a man's height, may perhaps make your friend wander in gathering of Berries till he cannot recover himself without your help.

To have occasion to exercise within your Orchard, it shall be a pleasure to have a bowling-Alley, or rather (which is more manly, and more healthful) a pair of Buts, to stretch your Arms.

Rosemary and sweet Eglantine are seemly Ornaments about a Door or Window, and so is Woodbine...

And in mine own opinion, I could highly commend your Orchard, if either through it, or hard by it, there should run a pleasant River with silver streams, you might sit in your Mount, and angle a peckled Trout, sleighty Eel, or some other dainty Fish. Or Moats, whereon you may row with a Boat, and fish with Nets...

A Vine overshadowing a seat, is very comely, though her Grapes with us ripen slowly.

One chief grace that adorns an Orchard, I cannot let slip: a brood of Nightingales, who with several notes and tunes, with a strong delightsome voice out of a weak body, will bear you company night and day. She loves (and lives in) hots of woods in her heart. She will help you to cleanse your trees of Caterpillars, and all noysome worms and flies. The gentle Robin-red-brest will help her, and in winter in the coldest storms will keep apart. Neither will the silly Wren be behind in Summer, with her distinct whistle, (like a sweet Recorder) to chear your spirits.

WILLIAM LAWSON (1553–1635)

*A New Orchard & Garden*

# *Villa Medici*

### . . .

AFTER DINNER THE four gentlemen and a guide took post horses to go and see a place of the duke's called Castello. The house has nothing worth while about it; but there are various things about the gardens. The whole estate is situated on the slope of a hill, so that the straight walks are all on a slope, but a soft and easy one; the cross walks are straight and level. One sees there many arbors, very thickly interwoven and covered with all kinds of odoriferous trees such as cedars, cypresses, orange trees, lemon trees, and olive trees, the branches so joined and interlaced that it is easy to see that the sun at its greatest strength could not get in; and copses of cypress and of those other trees disposed in order so close to each other that there is room for only three or four people to pass abreast. There is a big reservoir, among other things, in the middle of which you see a natural-looking artificial rock, and it seems all frozen over, by means of that material with which the duke has covered his grottoes at Pratolino; and above the rock is a large bronze statue of a very old hoary man seated on his rear with his arms crossed, from all over whose beard, forehead, and hair water flows incessantly, drop by drop, representing sweat and tears; and the fountain has no other conduit than that.

Elsewhere they had the very amusing experience of seeing what I have noted above; for as they were walking about the garden and looking at its curiosities, the gardener left their company for this purpose; and as they were in a certain spot contemplating certain marble statues, there spurted up under their feet and between their legs,

Giambologna's *Colossus* at Medici's Pratolino in Italy

through an infinite number of tiny holes, jets of water so minute that they were almost invisible, imitating supremely well the trickle of fine rain, with which they were completely sprinkled by the operation of some underground spring which the gardener was working more than two hundred paces from there, with such artifice that from there on the outside he made these spurts of water rise and fall as he pleased, turning and moving them just as he wanted. This same game is found here in several places.

They also saw the master fountain, which issues from a conduit in two very big bronze effigies, of which the lower holds the other in his arms and is squeezing him with all his might; the other half fainting, his head thrown back, seems to spurt this water forcibly out of his mouth; and it shoots out with such power that the stream of water rises thirty-seven fathoms above the height of these figures, which are at least twenty feet high. There is also a chamber among the branches of an evergreen tree, but much richer than any other that they had seen; for it is all filled out with the live green branches of the tree, and on all sides this chamber is so closed in by this verdure that there is no view out except through a few apertures that must be opened up by pushing aside the branches here and there; and in the center, through a concealed pipe, a jet of water rises right in this chamber through the center of a small marble table. Water music is also made here, but they could not hear it, for it was late for people who had to get back to town. They also saw the duke's escutcheon here high over a gateway, very well-formed of some branches of trees fostered and maintained in their natural strength by fibers that one can barely discern. They were here in the most unpropitious season for gardens, and were all the more amazed. There is also a handsome grotto, where you see all sorts of animals represented to the life, spouting the water of these fountains, some by the beak, some by the wing, some by the claw or ear or the nostril.

MICHEL DE MONTAIGNE (1533–92)

*Travel Journal*

## *Turkish Gardens*

. . .

I AM AT this present moment writing in a house situated on the banks
of the Hebrus, which runs under my chamber window. My garden is
full of all cypress trees, upon the branches of which several couple of
true turtles are saying soft things to one another from morning till
night. How naturally do *boughs* and *vows* come into my mind, at this
minute? and must not you confess, to my praise, that 'tis more than an
ordinary discretion that can resist the wicked suggestions of poetry, in
a place where truth, for once, furnishes all the ideas of pastoral. The
summer is already far advanced in this part of the world; and, for some
miles round Adrianople, the whole ground is laid out in gardens, and
the banks of the rivers are set with rows of fruit-trees, under which
all the most considerable Turks divert themselves every evening, not
with walking, that is not one of their pleasures; but a set party of them
chuse out a green spot, where the shade is very thick, and, there they
spread a carpet, on which they sit drinking their coffee, and are generally attended by some slave with a fine voice, or that plays on some
instrument. Every twenty paces you may see one of these little compa-
nies listening to the dashing of the river; and this taste is so universal,
that the very gardeners are not without it. I have often seen them and
their children sitting on the banks of the river, and playing on a rural
instrument, perfectly answering the description of the ancient *fistula*,
being composed of unequal reeds, with a simple, but agreeable softness in the sound.

LADY MARY WORTLEY MONTAGU (1689–1762)

*Letter*

*My Garden in the Wilderness*

. . .

*I know not how it is with you*
*I love the first and last—*
*The whole field of the present view,*
*The whole flow of the past.*
*Our lives and every day and hour*
*One symphony appear,*
*One road, one garden, every flower,*
*And every bramble dear.*
*R.L.S. [Robert Louis Stevenson]*

THE CHANDAN [Indian sandalwood] trees have just finished flowering and we breathe freely again. I am not sure that I should have chosen them for my garden, but long ago some one planted a group outside our gates and we allow them to remain, in spite of the disadvantage they entail in March and in October, when for two days the house and garden are permeated and rendered almost uninhabitable by the pungent scent of their blossoms. But it is a cleanly odour, with an aromatic suggestion of health, almost like that of pine trees, or eucalyptus, and they are the quaintest trees I have ever seen, regular fairy tale trees

with gnarled trunks and straight branches that grow stiffly upwards, and covered with precise bunches of dark green leaves. They suggest a decorative frieze by Walter Crane, and when I stand under them and look up into their branches, I seem to have left the common workaday world far behind me. And yet it is all around me, for the group marks the point at which the road branches, and, round the tank at the end of my garden, disappears from my view. I am glad to lose sight of it, for it is not a pleasant road, being deep in dust in summer and in mud in the rains, and down it come creaking carts, and harassed bullocks, and overladen pack ponies, that give me a pain in my heart.

In my garden there is a green refuge from the dust and glare outside. Behind the fern house the ground rises to the bank, and there, shaded by teak trees and closed in by a shrubbery, I have placed a seat. Even on hot mornings it is cool here, and I bring the dogs and a pretence of needlework and sit watching the casuarina trees balancing their delicate spires against the pale turquoise sky. We have groups of casuarinas planted at each end of the bungalow, and the least wind causes them to sway and sigh with a sound as of waves on a pebbly shore. The dogs

are distinctly bored by my tendency to loiter. They long to be scampering down the dusty road and barking up into the twisted sissoo trees that border it, returning in mind the virulent abuse heaped on them by squirrels who sit in high places. But as dogs are the quintessence of politeness, they lie about with the air of attentive resignation that they know so well how to assume, and, I suppose, hope that their devotion will, in time, touch me into doing my obvious duty to them.

My shrubbery is a mixed one, for I have not yet learnt the true landscape gardener's art of massing colours. So hibiscus, scarlet and salmon and cream, jostles *Tecoma stans* with its lime-green foliage and bunches of yellow bells, and on the fern house roof a mass of heavenly purple contends wildly with the tawny *Bignonia venusta*. I shall never be a real gardener because I love flowers too much, all of them individually, no matter where they are. Real gardeners harden their hearts, they do not permit pirate poppies and petunias to live in their rose beds, and no real gardener would for a moment dream of allowing the all-conquering morning glory to behave so badly to the more delicate, legitimate creepers on the fern house. I wish morning glory had not such fierce, unpleasant ways; I feel helpless before it. It creeps in through the lattice-work of the fern house and tangles the young begonias and maidenhairs, and it gets through the roof and worries the plants in the hanging baskets, and clings to my hair when I pass through. Some day I think I shall plant morning glory next to *Beaumontia grandiflora,* and then we shall see what happens. But perhaps beaumontia is too dignified to contend with a mere weed; there is something regal about the plant as there is about its name, a name I love to repeat to myself, it has so noble a sound. I have a sense of being honoured when, in February, the beaumontia gives me her great white, faintly scented blossoms for the yellow Doultonware bowls in my drawing-room. Perhaps it is because she flowers only then, and not, as many shrubs in India appear to do, whenever the fancy takes them. We have a coquettish kind of Jessamine tree that is always taking us by surprise, and bursting into a wild revel of blossom on the excuse of a casual shower.

KATHLEEN L. MURRAY, 1913
*My Garden in the Wilderness*

IN THE GARDEN

# A Child's Delight

. . .

THE CHILDREN'S GARDENS are very amusing... Aileen's garden was dull but tidy and fairly full. Sylvia's garden was rather wayward, Barbara's absolutely neglected, Aubrey's garden, aged 4 is really wonderful, he watches things grow, knows the names of all his plants and is thrilled and thrilling over it, so wise and sensible, picks off dead things, weeds, waters, propagates with sense and care. He has a row of sweet peas and roared with laughter at the idea of their climbing sticks, he put them in under protest, now in transport of delight, they climb! The lawn is covered with guinea pigs. I do wish we could have a garden and a country house and if only we could do that combined with sea and river it would be perfect.

EDWIN LUTYENS (1869–1944)

*Letter to his wife, Lady Emily Lutyens, July 24, 1904*

< Jesse Wilcox Smith (1863–1935) was the premier female American illustrator of her day.

IF I HAD a garden. Now, as it so happens I no longer have a garden. It isn't so terrible not to have a garden. It would be serious if the future garden, whose reality matters little, were beyond my grasp. It is not. A certain crackling of seeds in their paper packets is all it takes to sow the air. A seed of love-in-a-mist is black, brilliant as a hundred fleas, and, if heated, will smell of apricots for a long time, a quality it does not pass on to its flower. I shall sow love-in-a-mist when, in the garden of tomorrow, dreams, plans, and recollection have taken, have taken hold in the form of what I once owned and of what I am now banking on. To be sure, the hepaticas there will be blue, for the winy pink ones try my patience. Blue, and in sufficient numbers to edge the circular flower bed ("All the flowers beds must be round . . . ") that raises Dielytras to become *pendeloques,* weigelas, and double deutzias. The only pansies I shall have are those that look like Henry VIII— broad-faced, bearded, and mustachioed; some saxifrage, only if, one fine summer evening, when I politely offer them a lighted match, they respond with their harmless little burst of gas . . .

An arbor? Of course I shall have an arbor! I still have an arbor or two in me. The dragon-tongued, violet cobaea, the Polygonum, and the oar-driven melon must have a trellis perch . . . "Oar-driven melon"? Why not "motor-driven squash"? Because the melon I am talking about paddles and plies its way up any support just like a simple pea, leaving in its wake little green-and-white melons, sweet and bursting with flavor. (See the writings of Mme Millet-Robinet.)

If the lovers of horticultural novelties were to banish all the old love-lies-bleeding, I of course would take several in, if only to give them back their old name: nuns' disciplines. They will get on well with the feathery pampas grass, a decent sort, not too smart, who spends the winter on either side of the fireplace in cone-shaped vases.

Come summer, we will jilt the pampas grass and in its vases plant the suffocating white lily, more imperious than orange blossoms, more passionate than the tuberose; lilies that ascend the stair at midnight and seek us out in our deepest sleep.

If it is a garden in Brittany—how I love my ideal parterre plumed with points "ifs"—daphne... Must we call it daphne, or *"bois gentil,"* this small, concealed flower, immense by virtue of its fresh, noble scent, which breaks on the Breton winter air as early as January? In the showers that come with the tide from the west, a bush of *"bois gentil"* seems soused with perfumes. If I plant myself at the edge of a lake, I shall have, besides the dense shrubbery the deceased Old Gentleman used to train, I shall have Chimonanthus in water, in daphne's stead. The Chimonanthus, a December flower, has all the color and brightness of a cork shaving. It has one distinction, which is sure to give it away. In one place in Limousin, where I was unaware of its presence, in snowy weather I sensed, sought, and found it in the icy air, guided by its fragrance. On its branch it is dingy and dull, but gifted with great powers of seduction—when I think of Chimonanthus I think of nightingales. So, I shall have Chimonanthus... Don't I already?

I shall have many others, verbena rosettes, Aristolochia pipes, thrift tufts, Maltese cross crosses, lupine spikes, and moonflower insomniacs, Agrostic nebulae, and vanilla pinks, St.-John's-cane to help me along the final steps I travel, and asters to star my nights. A Campanula, a thousand Campanulas, to ring in the dawn at the same time the cock crows; a dahlia gadrooned like a Clouet strawberry; a digitalis so that the fox will have gloves—or so claims its common name; a Julienne, and not, as you might think, diced into the soup, but as a border! A border, I'm telling you, a border. Lobelias as a border, too, whose blue neither sky nor sea can rival. As for honeysuckle, I'll pick the most frail, which grows weak and wan for being so odoriferous. . . Last of all, I must have a magnolia that is a good layer, all covered with its white eggs as Easter approaches; a wisteria that, abandoning its long flowers drop by drop, turns the terrace into a purple lake. And lady's-slippers, enough to shoe the whole house. Don't offer me any rose laurel, I want only roses and laurel.

My choice does not mean that, once assembled, the flowers I have named will please the eye. And besides, I've forgotten some. But there's no rush. I am heeling them in, some in my memory, others in my imagination. Where, by the Grace of God, they still find the rich soil, the slightly bitter waters, the warmth and the gratitude that will perhaps keep them from dying.

COLETTE (1873–1954)

*"Flora and Pomona"*

274

# Angelo's Garden

. . .

*Angelo created gardens outside his makeshift shelter at*
*Pier 84 on the Hudson River in New York City.*

OUTSIDE MY HOUSE I have two gardens. It's not garden actually, no flowers or tomatoes or eggplants. It's a toy garden. I got a gorilla, Godzilla, a Barbie doll, and lotsa, lotsa toys. A lot of people come by over here. They just play with a bunch of knickknacks. They come over here and say, where did you get all this stuff? I say, I didn't buy them. The people that came over here they put them in there. It's like a museum. They come and say, "Do you still want the little toy, I give it to you?" And... nobody touches it. The garden it's got a snake fence, snakes take care of things, see I found that. And I found stones to make an edge for the garden...

In the summertime I go swimming a lot. In the eleven years I've been living on the pier over here, I've saved eleven lives and lost two. Last year they were fixing the pier over here, across the street from the hospital... [someone] fell in the river... I had to let him go. He tried to grab me, and I kick, you know, because he tried to grab me, and if I did not let go, we'd both be dead. A little Puerto Rican girl, seven years old, fell in three weeks ago. It was February 29th, and I jump in the water and saved her. But thank God, she spoke English. I said, "Honey, put your arm around my neck, and don't let go." And then when she comes again she gives me a name, she calls me Papi. I guess that means father or grandfather in Spanish. Her father, he's a junkie, they were doing drugs. They didn't care when they came out here [with her]. They were screaming, and I said, "What are you worried about now? I saved the girl." They didn't even stop to say thank you. But the little girl last week, seven years old, she come over here by herself... and she brought me a little Barbie doll. See, it's in the garden.

DIANA BALMORI AND MARGARET MORTON, 1993
*Transitory Gardens, Uprooted Lives*

## A Garden Contained

. . .

WERE I EMPLY'D a Garden to contrive,
Wherein to plant each beauteous Vegetive;
First then my Walls so fashioned should be,
Each side and part the Sun each Day should see
So that the Fruit within, or outside set
An equal share of's ripening Beams should get.
A Fountain in the midst should so be plac'd
By which the Plot shou'd not be only grac'd,

But that one spring should force the Water out
In seeming Show'rs of Rain, each part about
Farther or shorter Distance, more or less,
Water to big, or smaller drops shall press,
As the inclosed Plants or Flowers require;
Gentle or fiercer Rain, to your desire.
Invented Shades to keep out Sol's South Flames,
And apt Reflections to enforce his Beams,
As nature of each Plant shall want his Aid,
Or those that by his heat may be dismay'd,
Assisting Nature by industrious Art;
To perfect every Plant in every part,
But not like some, whose crimes do rise so high,
Boldly to pull down Heaven's Deity.
I hate that so sordid Ignorance doth dispence
With making Nature God, slight Providence,
But let each Vegetive best ordred prove
Such Letters, so may spell the God above,
That Men may read him thence, and make each Clod
Speak God of Nature, make not Nature God:
But Blaz'ner of's wise Providence and Power,
First made, then so preserves each Plant and Flower.

SAMUEL GILBERT (D. 1692)

*The Florist's Vade Mecum*

## ACKNOWLEDGMENTS

ALBERTUS MAGNUS: from *On Vegetables and Plants*. Translation copyright © 1981 John Harvey. My thanks to the Harvey family for permission to use the extract from John Harvey's *Mediaeval Gardens*, 1981. JOHN ALCOCK: from *In a Desert Garden* by John Alcock. Copyright © 1997 by John Alcock. Used by permission of W.W. Norton & Company, Inc. GAIL ANDERSON-DARGATZ: excerpted from *A Recipe for Bees* by Gail Anderson-Dargatz. Copyright © 1998 by Gail Anderson-Dargatz. Reprinted by permission of Knopf Canada. From *A Recipe for Bees* by Gail Anderson-Dargatz, copyright © 1999 by Gail

< In the 1880s, William Morris revived the intricate art
of medieval Arras tapestry at his workshop at Merton Abbey.

THE AUTHOR AND THE PUBLISHER EXTEND

THEIR THANKS TO THE FOLLOWING IMAGE COLLECTIONS:

Brooklyn Museum/Corbis: p. 156

The Bridgeman Art Library/Getty Images: pp. 128 and 168

Mary Evans Picture Library: pp. 4, 7, 15, 26, 28, 46, 48, 60,
65, 82, 87, 112, 123, 137, 146, 162, 176, 184, 204, 211, 216, 236,
242, 251, and 255

Mary Evans Picture Library/Beranger Collection: p. 91

Mary Evans Picture Library/Illustrated London News Ltd:
pp. 78 and 88

Photography Collection, Miriam and Ira D. Wallach Division
of Art, Prints and Photographs, The New York Public Library,
Astor, Lenox, and Tilden Foundations: p. 226

Picture Collection, The New York Public Library, Astor, Lenox,
and Tilden Foundations: pp. 51, 151, 261, 270, 275, and 296

Rare Books and Special Collections, McGill University
Library: p. 200

Slavic and Baltic Division, The New York Public Library,
Astor, Lenox, and Tilden Foundations: p. 196

Spencer Collection, The New York Public Library, Astor,
Lenox, and Tilden Foundations: pp. 8 and 19

# SOURCES

Albertus Magnus. *On Vegetables and Plants*. Translated and quoted in *Mediaeval Gardens* by John Harvey. London: Batsford, 1981.

Alcock, John. *In a Desert Garden: Love and Death Among the Insects*. London and New York: W.W. Norton, 1997.

Anderson-Dargatz, Gail. *A Recipe for Bees*. Toronto: Alfred A. Knopf, 1998.

*Arabian Nights Entertainments*. Translated by Dr. Jonathan Scott. London: Pickering and Chatto, 1890.

Arnim, Elizabeth von. *Elizabeth and Her German Garden*. London: Macmillan and Co., Limited, 1898.

Austen, R.A. *The Spiritual Use of an Orchard*. Oxford: Thomas Robinson, 1653.

Babur. *The Baburnama: Memoirs of Babur, Prince and Emperor*. Edited and translated by Wheeler M. Thackston. Washington, D.C.: Smithsonian Institution, 1996.

Balmori, Diana, and Margaret Morton. *Transitory Gardens, Uprooted Lives*. New Haven and London: Yale University Press, 1993.

Baudry. Quoted in *Jardins de Touraine* by L. Berluchon. Tours, France: Chez
   Arrault et Cie, 1940. Translated and quoted by Patrick Taylor in "France: The
   Middle Ages," in *Oxford Companion to the Garden*, edited by Patrick Taylor.
   Oxford: Oxford University Press, 2006.

Bible (King James Version). Genesis 2:8–15.

Bible (King James Version). The Song of Solomon 4:12–16.

Blaikie, Thomas. *Diary of a Scotch Gardener at the French Court at the End of
   the Eighteenth Century.* Edited by Francis Birrell. London: Routledge &
   Sons, 1931.

Boccaccio, Giovanni. *The Decameron.* Translated by J.M. Rigg. London:
   A.H. Bullen, 1903.

Bowles, E.A. *My Garden in Summer.* London: T.C. and E.C. Jack, 1914.

Buchan, William. "On improving the gardens of cottages, as practised by the late
   Lord Cawdor at Stackpole Court, in Pembrokeshire." *Gardener's Magazine*,
   vol. 1 (1826): 275–76.

Cao Xueqin. *Red Chamber Dream (Hong Lou Meng).* Unpublished translation
   by Bramwell Seaton Bonsall. Hong Kong: Hong Kong University Libraries,
   2005.

Čapek, Karel. *The Gardener's Year.* Translated by M. and R. Weatherall. London:
   George Allen & Unwin Ltd., 1931.

Cather, Willa. *My Ántonia.* Boston, New York: Houghton Mifflin, 1918.

Chudley, Carol Graham, and Dorothy Field. *Between Gardens: Observations
   on Gardening, Friendship, and Disability.* Vancouver: Polestar Book
   Publishers, 1999.

Colette, Sidonie-Gabrielle. "Flora and Pomona." In *Flowers and Fruit*, translated
   by Matthew Ward and edited by Robert Phelps. New York: Farrar, Straus and
   Giroux, 1986.

Cooper, Guy, and Gordon Taylor. *Gardens for the Future: Gestures against the
   Wild.* New York: The Monacelli Press, 2000.

Dickens, Charles. "London Recreations." In *Sketches by Boz: Illustrative of
   Everyday Life and Everyday People.* London: Chapman and Hall, 1836.

Evelyn, George. Letter to his brother John, December 12, 1650. British Library
   Add. MS 78303, f. 49. Quoted by Frances Harris in "'My Most Cherished

Place on Earth': John Evelyn and Wotton" in *A Celebration of John Evelyn: Proceedings of a Conference to Mark the Tercentenary of His Death*, edited by Mavis Batey. Dorking: Surrey Gardens Trust, 2007.

Flaubert, Gustave. *Bouvard and Pécuchet*, 1881.

Gilbert, Samuel. *The Florist's Vade Mecum*. London: for T. Simmons, 1682.

Gilpin, William. *Rygate–Dorking, The Rookery, August 24, 1768*. Unpublished manuscript at the Bodleian Library, Oxford. MS. Eng. Misc. e. 522. Reprinted in *Pursuit of the Picturesque: William Gilpin's Surrey Excursion. The Places He Passed and Their Claims to Fame 1724–1804*, edited by Joan Percy. Dorking: Surrey Gardens Trust, 2001.

Goethe, Johann Wolfgang von. *Elective Affinities*. Translated by Victoria C. Woodhull. Boston: D.W. Niles, 1872.

Goodman, Richard. *French Dirt*. Chapel Hill, NC: Algonquin Books, 1991.

Greer, Germaine (Rose Blight). *The Revolting Garden*. London: Private Eye, 1979.

Hardy, Thomas. *Tess of the D'Urbervilles*. Leipzig: Tauchnitz, 1892.

Hawthorne, Nathaniel. *Mosses from an Old Manse*. New York: Wiley and Putnam, 1846.

Hole, S. Reynolds. *Our Gardens*. London: J.M. Dent & Co., 1899.

Homer. *The Odyssey*. Translated by Samuel Butler. London: A.C. Fifield, 1900.

*Interpretation of the Holy Qur'an*. English text by A. Yusuf Ali, 1938.

*Ishtar and Izdubar: The Epic of Babylon*. Translated by Leonidas Le Cenci Hamilton. London and New York: W.H. Allen & Co., 1884.

Jahangir. *Memoirs of the Emperor Jahangueir*. Translated by David Price. London: Oriental Translation Committee, 1829.

Jansson, Tove. *The Summer Book*. Translated by Thomas Teal. New York: Random House, 1974.

Jarman, Derek. *Derek Jarman's Garden*. London: Thames & Hudson, 1995.

Jekyll, Gertrude. *Colour in the Flower Garden*. London: Country Life, 1908.

Ji Cheng. *The Craft of Gardens*. Translated by Alison Hardie. New Haven and London: Yale University Press, 1988.

Kálidása. *Sakoontalá*. Translated by Sir Monier Monier-Williams. In *Hindu Literature*, edited by Epiphanius Wilson. New York: P.F. Collier & Son, 1900.

Keane, Marc Peter. *The Art of Setting Stones: & Other Writings from the Japanese Garden*. Berkeley, CA: Stone Bridge Press, 2002.

Keane, Molly (M.J. Farrell). *Full House*. London: Collins, 1935.

Kincaid, Jamaica. *My Garden (Book)*. New York: Farrar, Straus and Giroux, 1999.

Kogawa, Joy. *Obasan*. Toronto: Lester & Orpen Dennys, 1983.

Lane, Patrick. *There Is a Season*. Toronto: McClelland & Stewart, 2004. Published in the United States as *What the Stones Remember*. Boston: Trumpeter Books, 2005.

Lawson, William. *A New Orchard & Garden*. Originally published 1618. Facsimile edition. London: The Cresset Press Limited, 1927.

Lee, Laurie. *Cider with Rosie*. London: The Hogarth Press, 1959.

Lewis, Matthew. *The Monk*. 1796.

Lorris, Guillaume de, and Jean de Meun. *The Romance of the Rose*. Translated by F.S. Ellis. London: J.M. Dent & Co., 1900.

Loudon, John Claudius. *The Villa Gardener: Comprising the Choice of a Suburban Villa Residence; The Laying Out, Planting and Culture of the Garden and Grounds and The Management of the Villa Farm, Including the Dairy and Poultry Yard, and More Particularly for the Use of Ladies*. London: Wm. S. Orr & Co, 1850.

Louis XIV of France (attrib.). "Manière de montrer les jardins de Versailles." c. 1694. Translated by Christopher Thacker. *Garden History*, vol. 1 no. 1 (1972): 49–69.

Lutyens, Edwin. Letter to his wife, Emily Lutyens, July 24, 1904. In *The Letters of Edwin Lutyens to his Wife, Lady Emily*, edited by Clayre Percey and Jane Ridley. London: Collins, 1985.

Malinowski, Bronislaw. *Coral Gardens and Their Magic*. London: George Allen & Unwin Ltd., 1935.

Mansfield, Katherine. "The Garden-Party." In *The Garden Party, and Other Stories*. New York: Alfred A. Knopf, 1922.

Maryon, Maud. *How the Garden Grew*. London: Longman's, Green, and Co., 1900.

Milne, A.A. *If I May*. London: Methuen Young Books, 1920.

Mina, Denise. *Field of Blood*. London: Bantam, 2005.

Mitchell, John Hanson. *The Wildest Place on Earth: Italian Gardens and the Invention of Wilderness*. Washington, D.C.: Counterpoint, 2001.

Mitchell, W.O. *Roses Are Difficult Here*. Toronto: McClelland & Stewart, 1990.

Montagu, Lady Mary Wortley. *Letters of the Honourable Lady Wortley Montagu Written During Her Travels in Europe, Asia and Africa*. London: Thomas Martin, 1790.

Montagu, Mrs. Elizabeth. Letter, 1744. Quoted in *A Celebration of Gardens*, edited by Roy Strong. London: HarperCollins, 1991.

Montaigne, Michel de. *The Complete Works of Montaigne: Essays, Travel Journal, Letters*. Translated by Donald Frame. Palo Alto, CA: Stanford University Press, 1943.

Murray, Kathleen L. *My Garden in the Wilderness*. London: W. Thacker & Co., 1913.

Ondaatje, Michael. *Running in the Family*. Toronto: McClelland & Stewart, 1982.

Paul, William. "On Colour in the Tree Scenery of our Gardens, Parks & Pleasure Grounds." Address to the Horticultural Congress, Oxford, July 21, 1870, and Cottage Gardens Associations. Reprinted in *The Garden*, December 9, 1882.

Phillpotts, Eden. *My Garden*. London: Country Life, 1906.

Platter, Thomas the Younger. *Thomas Platter's Travels in England 1599*. Translated by Clare Williams. London: J. Cape, 1937.

Pliny the Younger. Letter to Domitius Apollinaris. In *The Letters of the Younger Pliny*, translated by Betty Radice. London, New York, Victoria, Toronto, Auckland: Penguin Books, 1963.

Pollan, Michael. *Second Nature: A Gardener's Education*. New York: Grove Press, 1991.

Pope, Alexander. *The Guardian*, September 29, 1713.

Porter, Sir Robert Ker. *Travels in Georgia, Persia, Armenia, Ancient Babylonia, &c. &c. during the years 1817, 1818, 1819, 1820*. London: Longman, Hurst, Rees, Orme, and Brown, 1821–22.

Proust, Marcel. *Swann's Way*. Translated by C.K. Scott Moncrieff. New York: Henry Holt and Company, 1922.

"Qi Biaojia's 'Footnotes to Allegory Mountain': Introduction and Translation." By Duncan Campbell in *Studies in the History of Gardens and Designed Landscapes*, vol. 19 no. 3/4 (1999): 246–47.

Raver, Anne. *Deep in the Green: An Exploration of Country Pleasures*. New York: Alfred A. Knopf, 1995.

Rosa. "My Flowers." *The Cottage Gardener*, vol. 1 no. 3 (1848): 29.

Rousseau, Jean-Jacques. *Julie, ou La Nouvelle Héloïse*. In *The Collected Writings of Rousseau*, translated by Philip Steward and Jean Vaché and edited by Roger D. Masters and Christopher Kelly. Hanover, NH, and London: University Press of New England, 1997.

Sheeler, Jessie, and Andrew Lawson. *Little Sparta: The Garden of Ian Hamilton Finlay*. London: Frances Lincoln, 2003.

Shikibu, Murasaki. *Tale of Genji*. Translated by Edward G. Seidensticker. New York: Alfred A. Knopf, 1976.

Sitwell, Osbert. *The Scarlet Tree, Being the second volume of Left Hand, Right Hand!* London: Macmillan & Co. Ltd., 1946.

St. Aubin de Terán, Lisa. *The Hacienda: My Venezuelan Years*. London: Virago, 1997.

Stoppard, Tom. *Arcadia*. London: Faber and Faber, 1993.

Sutra on the Buddha of Eternal Life. *Buddhist Mahâyâna Texts, Part II, The Larger Sukhâvatî-Vyûha. The Sacred Books of the East*, volume XLIX. Translated by E.B. Cowell, F. Max Müller, and J. Takakusu. Oxford: The Clarendon Press, 1894.

Tachibana no Toshitsuna. *Sakuteiki, Visions of the Japanese Garden: A Modern Translation of Japan's Gardening Classic* by Jirō Takei and Marc P. Keane. Boston: Tuttle Publishing, 2001.

Thackeray, William Makepeace. *Vanity Fair*. London: Punch Magazine, 1847–48.

Thaxter, Celia. *An Island Garden*. Boston and New York: Houghton, Mifflin & Co., 1894.

Thompson, Flora. *Lark Rise*. Oxford: Oxford University Press, 1939.

Thoreau, Henry David. *Walden*. Boston: Houghton, Mifflin, 1854.

Walafrid Strabo. *Hortulus or, The Little Garden: A Ninth Century Poem*. Translated by Richard Stanton Lambert. Wembley, Middlesex, England: Stanton Press, 1923.

Welty, Eudora. "A Curtain of Green." In *A Curtain of Green*. New York: Harcourt, Brace and World Inc., 1941.

Werner, E.T.C. *Myths and Legends of China*. London, Bombay, Sydney: George G. Harrap & Co. Ltd., 1922.

Xenophon. *The Economist*. Translated by H.G. Dakyns. London: Macmillan, 1890.

Zhu Changwen. "The Record of the Joy Garden." Quoted in *Painting and Private Life in Eleventh-Century China: Mountain Villa by Li Gonglin* by Robert E. Harrist, Jr. Princeton: Princeton University Press, 1998.

# INDEX OF AUTHORS